Taxcafe.co.uk Tax Guides

Non-Resident & Offshore Tax Planning

By Lee Hadnum LLB ACA CTA

Important Legal Notices:

TAXCafe™

TAX GUIDE - "Non-Resident and Offshore Tax Planning"

Published by:
Taxcafe UK Limited
214 High St
Kirkcaldy KY1 1JT
Tel: (0044) 01592 560081
Email: team@taxcafe.co.uk

Fifth Edition, April 2006

ISBN 1 904608 36 1

Copyright

Copyright © Lee Hadnum. All rights reserved.

Trademarks

The logo "TAXCafe™" is a trademark of Taxcafe UK Limited. All other logos, trademarks, names and logos in this Tax Guide may be trademarks of their respective owners.

Disclaimer

1. Please note that this tax guide is intended as **general guidance only** for individual readers and does NOT constitute accountancy, tax, investment or other professional advice. Taxcafe UK Limited and the author accept no responsibility or liability for loss which may arise from reliance on information contained in this tax guide.

2. Please note that tax legislation, the law and practices by government and regulatory authorities (for example, HM Revenue and Customs) are constantly changing and the information contained in this tax guide is only correct as at the date of publication. We therefore recommend that for accountancy, tax, investment or other professional advice, you consult a suitably qualified accountant, tax specialist, independent financial adviser, or other professional adviser. Please also note that your personal circumstances may vary from the general examples given in this tax guide and your professional adviser will be able to give specific advice based on your personal circumstances.

3. This tax guide covers UK taxation mainly and any references to 'tax' or 'taxation' in this tax guide, unless the contrary is expressly stated, are to UK taxation only. Please note that references to the 'UK' do not include the Channel Islands or the Isle of Man. Addressing all foreign tax implications is beyond the scope of this tax guide.

4. Whilst in an effort to be helpful, this tax guide may refer to general guidance on matters other than UK taxation, Taxcafe UK Limited and the author are not experts in these matters and do not accept any responsibility or liability for loss which may arise from reliance on such information contained in this tax guide.

5. Please note that Taxcafe UK Limited has relied wholly upon the expertise of the author in the preparation of the content of this tax guide. The author is not an employee of Taxcafe UK Limited but has been selected by Taxcafe UK Limited using reasonable care and skill to write the content of this tax guide.

Other Taxcafe guides by the same author

Using a Company to Save Tax

The World's Best Tax Havens

How to Avoid Tax on Your Stock Market Profits

Selling a Sole Trader Business

About the Author

Lee Hadnum is a key member of the Taxcafe team. Apart from authoring a number of our tax guides, he also provides personalised tax advice through our popular Question & Answer Service, a role he carries out with a great deal of enthusiasm and professionalism.

Lee is a rarity among tax advisers having both legal AND chartered accountancy qualifications. After qualifying as a prize winner in the Institute of Chartered Accountants entrance exams, he went on to become a Chartered Tax Adviser (CTA).

Having worked in Ernst & Young's tax department for a number of years, Lee decided to start his own tax consulting firm, specialising in capital gains tax, inheritance tax and business tax planning.

He also tutors at a number of accountancy colleges in the north-west of England.

Whenever he has spare time Lee enjoys DIY, walking and travelling.

Nick Braun, Managing Director, Taxcafe UK Limited

Contents

Chapter 1

Introduction

This guide is designed to help those living or working abroad pay less tax on their UK income and investments. It also contains important information for those who live in the UK but wish to use the offshore tax rules to shelter their income and gains from the taxman.

This is an important and sophisticated area of tax planning. Moving yourself or your assets abroad is in many respects the ultimate form of tax avoidance and in some cases it is possible to reduce your tax bill to zero. However, there are also many traps to avoid and pitfalls to negotiate.

This publication highlights some of the key tax-planning opportunities and dangers, focusing on the UK's four major taxes: income tax, capital gains tax, inheritance tax and corporation tax.

Throughout we have tried to keep tax jargon to a minimum and illustrate the main points with examples.

A significant portion of the guide is devoted to the potential emigrant – individuals who are considering moving overseas and have heard that this may bring with it substantial tax benefits.

We look at the tax-saving opportunities, as well as the practical steps and dangers to bear in mind, when considering a move abroad.

In Chapter 2 we explain the concept of 'non residence' which has a huge effect on the amount of income tax and capital gains tax you pay. We also explain the concept of 'domicile' as there are a number of special rules for individuals who are UK resident but not UK domiciled. Domicile is also crucial when it comes to inheritance tax planning.

In Chapter 3 we list the steps you need to take to convince the taxman that you are non-resident and discuss some of the traps the authorities have set to catch 'phoney emigrants'.

Chapters 4, 5 and 6 take a detailed look at income tax, capital gains tax and inheritance tax-planning strategies for non-residents. The information contained in these chapters is extremely important for any would-be tax exile or emigrant and should be read carefully.

In Chapter 7 we focus our attention on non-domiciled people living and working in the UK and explain how they can use their special status to obtain tax savings.

In Chapter 8 we look at the income tax, capital gains tax and inheritance tax implications of working and travelling overseas as, aside from the 'permanent emigrant', many of you reading this may be considering an overseas posting. After reading this guide you should have a clear understanding of how working abroad will affect your UK tax position.

Chapter 9 explains how you can use a number of reliefs to avoid being taxed twice – once in the UK and again in another country.

Offshore trusts and offshore companies are sometimes viewed as the preserve of the very wealthy. This is not necessarily the case and we have outlined in Chapters 10 and 11 how these structures can help you save tax and how to avoid the detailed tax anti-avoidance rules.

Reducing tax on property investments is a top priority for many UK residents and non-residents. The guide contains numerous examples with a 'property theme' and in Chapter 12 we take a closer look at how non-resident and non-domiciled investors should structure their property purchases.

Your residence status is often the critical factor when it comes to paying both UK and foreign taxes. But what if you can avoid being resident in ANY country? In Chapter 13 we take a brief look at how you can become a 'tax nomad' and avoid both UK and overseas taxes.

Throughout this guide we have attempted to identify practical steps that can be taken to mitigate any UK tax, although the tax regime of any relevant overseas country should also be borne in mind. This is where double tax treaties come in. In Chapter 14 we explain the importance of these treaties in further detail.

Finally, Chapter 15 takes an in-depth look at buying property abroad and how to plan your affairs to avoid both UK and overseas income tax and capital gains tax.

We occasionally use some abbreviations. In particular, capital gains tax may be referred to as CGT, inheritance tax as IHT and HM Revenue and Customs as HMRC.

A lot of expat and offshore tax planning depends on getting dates and timing right, so many of the examples are based on specific tax years.

Remember that the UK tax year runs from April 6th to April 5th.

The tax year running from April 6th 2006 to April 5th 2007 may be referred to as the 2006/2007 tax year or just 2006/07.

Finally, remember that offshore tax planning is an extremely complex area and the relevant tax legislation, as well as HMRC's practices, can change quickly. You should never take any action until you have spoken to a suitably qualified professional who can advise you based on your personal circumstances.

Chapter 2

Residence, Ordinary Residence & Domicile

2.1   WHY DO RESIDENCE & DOMICILE MATTER?

The short answer is, they affect the amount of tax you have to pay.

UK residents who are also UK domiciled (we'll explain domicile later) have to pay UK income tax and capital gains tax on their 'worldwide income and gains'. In other words, no matter where in the world your assets are located or in what country your income is earned, it all falls into the UK tax net.

Those who are UK resident but non-UK domiciled are only subject to UK income tax on income from foreign assets when they bring it into the UK.

If you are a non-resident you do not have to pay UK tax on non-UK income. However, you still have to pay UK tax on your UK salary, business profits (if the business is carried out in the UK), pension income and investment income. There are, however, some special rules that can reduce the tax non-residents pay on some types of UK income.

Capital gains tax depends on both your residence and 'ordinary residence'. If you cease to be resident in the UK without also ceasing to be ordinarily resident here, you will remain liable to UK capital gains tax in respect of gains on your worldwide assets.

If an individual ceases to be both resident and ordinarily resident, he is outside the scope of UK capital gains tax, even on UK assets.

So clearly your residence and domicile have a huge effect on the size of your UK tax bill. The crucial question is how do you qualify for these reliefs and exemptions?

2.2 BECOMING NON-RESIDENT

There is no formal legal definition of 'residence'. Revenue's practice – based on a mixture of statute and court decisions – is to regard you as resident in the UK during a tax year if :

- You spend 183 days or more in the UK during the tax year, or

- Although here for less than 183 days, you have spent more than 90 days per year in the country over the past four years (taken as an average). You will then be classed as UK resident from the fifth year.

These rules have no statutory force and are guidance only.

For example, an individual who regularly returns to the UK for 87 days per tax year may still be regarded as UK resident.

This is a crucial point to remember. Although these limits are undoubtedly important, they are not the end of the matter. In one well-known case in 2005 it was decided that an airline pilot was UK resident, even though he spent less than 90 days in the UK.

In this case the taxman said that the 90-day limit was guidance only, and although the pilot spent less than 90 days per tax year in the UK he still had a house here and visited regularly. Therefore there was an 'ongoing connection' with the UK and the pilot had not provided enough evidence to indicate that the UK was no longer his home.

That's why I recommend that, if you want to establish non-residence, only minimal visits are made to the UK (particularly in the year of departure and the following year) and UK property should be sold or rented out on a long lease while you are overseas.

A person can also be resident in two countries at the same time. It is therefore not possible to escape UK residence by arguing that you are resident elsewhere.

It is important to note that UK residence is a question of fact and not intention. Therefore although you may intend to leave before the 183-day limit, if you are forced to remain in the UK as a result of exceptional circumstances you will nevertheless be regarded as UK resident.

(On a technical note, in strict terms when calculating the number of days an individual spends in the UK, the hours that he is in this country on the days of arrival and departure should be taken into account. However, in practice HMRC allows the days of arrival and departure to be ignored, although if the tax at stake is significant, it would be unwise to depend too heavily on this practice.)

2.3   THE IMPORTANCE OF 'ORDINARY RESIDENCE'

Even if you qualify as non-resident you may still fall into the taxman's clutches by being classified as UK ordinarily resident.

There is also no statutory test of ordinary residence. You will be classified as a UK ordinary resident if the UK is your 'normal place of residence'.

On leaving the country you will continue to be regarded as UK ordinary resident unless you go abroad with the intention of taking up permanent residence overseas.

Revenue and Customs normally interprets 'permanent' to mean three years or more.

It is therefore possible to be non-UK resident but UK ordinarily resident. This would occur, for example, where you go abroad for a long holiday and do not return to the UK during a particular tax year. You will continue to be classed as UK ordinary resident until you can show that you have taken up a permanent residence elsewhere.

The consequence of being classed as not UK ordinary resident is that you will not have to pay UK capital gains tax on your worldwide capital gains.

A person who is UK resident under the 183-day test may not necessarily be UK ordinary resident. Such a person would then have to pay tax on overseas income and gains that are brought into the UK (this applies for Commonwealth and Irish citizens).

However, a person who is UK resident as a result of the 90-day test would find it difficult to argue that he or she is not also UK ordinary resident and therefore worldwide income and gains would be taxed as they arise, not just when brought into the UK. This is because the visits over a number of tax years would be evidence of an ongoing connection with the UK which would indicate UK ordinary residence status.

One factor that is likely to be taken into account in assessing ordinary residence is whether you continue to own and occupy property in the UK – in particular, where the use or occupation of the property is combined with other factors, such as regular visits to the UK only slightly below the 90-day average. This will be persuasive evidence that you have not taken up a permanent residence elsewhere.

However, subject to this, a person who leaves the UK will cease to be UK ordinary resident if he or she establishes non-UK residence for three consecutive tax years.

2.4 RESIDENCE IN A NUTSHELL

As you can see, residence issues can be fairly complex. It is useful to consolidate the above before looking at the detailed rules:

- An individual who is UK resident/ordinarily resident and domiciled will be liable to UK tax on his/her worldwide income and gains.

- An individual who is UK resident/ordinarily resident but not UK domiciled will generally be liable to UK tax on overseas income/gains only when the income/proceeds are remitted to the UK. This is known as the remittance basis.

- An individual who is UK resident but not ordinarily resident will also be subject to the remittance basis for overseas income and gains (provided he or she is a Commonwealth or Irish citizen).

- An individual who is non-resident and not ordinarily resident will be liable to UK income tax on UK source income but will be exempt from UK capital gains tax on all assets (whether situated in the UK or overseas), except for assets used in a UK trade.

Example 1

John, who is UK domiciled, has purchased a holiday villa in Spain and intends to spend as much time there as possible.

John stays 10 months in the villa. In order to supplement his income he is renting out his property in the UK (through a letting agent) and will obtain a small part-time job in a Spanish wine factory, tasting local wines.

From a UK tax perspective he will be regarded as non-UK resident as he has exceeded the 183-day limit. Therefore:

- *His UK source income (in other words, rental income) will be subject to UK income tax.*

- *His overseas income (his income from his part-time job in Spain) will not be subject to UK taxation.*

If Spanish property prices were to suddenly increase, John may decide to take advantage of this and dispose of his Spanish villa in July 2006, for a healthy profit.

As he has not left the UK permanently and he has not yet been non-resident for three complete tax years, he is likely to still be regarded as UK ordinarily resident. This will mean that his profit from the sale of the Spanish villa will be subject to UK capital gains tax.

Note that if John cannot show that he has gone to Spain 'permanently' (for at least three years) or for another 'settled purpose' (for example, to establish a business in Spain) then the UK taxman may regard him as UK resident from the date of his departure. Revenue and Customs will then review the tax years he has spent out of the country after he has been overseas for three years. Therefore he should still be able to be classed as non-resident provided he satisfies the 90-day and 183-day limits.

Example 2

Johnny, of Australian domicile, makes regular visits to the UK to visit his friends in London. His visits to the UK over the past few tax years have been as follows:

2002/2003	*85 days*
2003/2004	*97 days*
2004/2005	*110 days*
2005/2006	*115 days*

His annual average visits are (85+97+110+115)/4 = 102 days.

He will therefore be regarded as UK resident from 6 April 2006 and subject to UK tax on his worldwide income and gains, although the remittance basis would apply to his overseas income and gains.

If he has a job in Australia he will not be subject to UK tax if he keeps the income out of the UK. However, to the extent that he brings it into the UK, eg for spending money during his visits, it will be subject to UK tax.

Any amounts that are taxed twice will be entitled to double tax relief (this is explained later in the guide).

It should be noted that if Johnny had any firm intentions, beginning with the commencement of his visits to the UK in 2002, that his visits would be on the above basis, then he would be regarded as UK resident from the date that these intentions were formed.

For example, if Johnny had declared in May 2002 that he would be making substantial visits to the UK in the following tax years and, for example, booked time off work to make the visits, he would be regarded as UK resident from this date.

2.5   WHY DOMICILE IS SO IMPORTANT

The concept of domicile is extremely important when it comes to both inheritance tax and overseas tax planning.

It's important to point out that your 'nationality' or 'citizenship' are NOT necessarily the same as your domicile.

You are normally domiciled in the country that you regard as your home – not the place where you happen to be temporarily living. Your domicile is, in a sense, the country that you regard as your true 'homeland' and has frequently been described as the country in which a person intends to die.

It is therefore possible for a person to live in the UK for 40 years yet still remain legally domiciled in another country. Losing your UK domicile is substantially more difficult than losing your UK resident status.

While it is possible to be resident in two countries at the same time, it is only possible to be domiciled in one.

There are three types of domicile:

1. Domicile of Origin

A domicile of origin is acquired when a person is born. Under normal circumstances this is the father's domicile at the date of the child's birth. If the parents are unmarried, it is the mother's domicile that matters.

A domicile of origin continues unless the individual acquires either a domicile of dependency or a domicile of choice (see below). This new domicile will remain in force unless it is abandoned, in which case the domicile of origin is revived.

2. Domicile of Choice

In order to acquire a domicile of choice, a person must voluntarily make a new territory his residence and intend to remain there for the rest of his days – unless and until something occurs to make him change his mind.

Obtaining a domicile of choice is primarily a question of intent. However, once such a domicile has been established it is relatively difficult to abandon. It would be necessary for an individual to cease to reside in the country of choice indefinitely. Later on in this guide we list some practical steps that can be taken to help establish a domicile of choice.

3. Domicile of Dependency

This type of domicile only applies to children under the age of 16. A child's domicile of origin is replaced by a domicile of dependency if there is a change in the father's domicile (mother's domicile in the case of unmarried couples). If this happens, the parent's domicile of choice becomes the child's domicile of dependency. The child keeps this domicile unless the child does not live in the territory and never intends to live there. In this case the child's domicile of origin revives.

Example

John was born in Latvia and is regarded as being of Latvian domicile. John went to live in France and successfully established France as his domicile of choice. His son Jack, who was born in Latvia, would also initially have a Latvian domicile of origin. However, he would 'inherit' his father's French domicile. This would become his domicile of dependency. If Jack intends to permanently return to Latvia on his 18th birthday and makes preparations for this, his domicile will revert to his domicile of origin. The domicile of dependency has essentially been changed – by indicating his intention to return to Latvia, the domicile of origin 'reasserts' itself.

2.6   WATCH OUT FOR THIS INHERITANCE TAX TRAP

Inheritance tax issues are dealt with later in the guide. However it is worth noting now that for inheritance tax purposes only there is the concept of 'deemed domicile'. Individuals are deemed to have a UK domicile:

- If they have been UK resident for 17 out of the last 20 years, or
- They have lost their UK domicile in the last three years.

Example

David was born in France, but has been living in the UK since 1960. He has always intended to return to France, and still regards France as his home. For income tax purposes, and under the general law, David is of French domicile.

However, for inheritance tax purposes, he is deemed UK domicile as he has lived in the UK since 1960 and would therefore have been resident for more than 17 years.

Therefore for inheritance tax purposes, David would be subject to UK inheritance tax on his worldwide estate. On his return to France, David would continue to be deemed UK domicile for inheritance tax purposes for three years after leaving the UK.

Chapter 3

How to Become Non-Resident

3.1 WHAT YOU STAND TO GAIN

Some people emigrate to soak up the sun and live in an exotic location. Others leave the country to escape the UK taxman. However, it is worth noting that tax rates in most industrialised countries are higher than those in the UK. Therefore, if you become non-resident to avoid tax, you may end up jumping out of the frying pan and into the fire!

To achieve a permanent reduction in tax it is often necessary to move to a tax haven or low tax jurisdiction such as Jersey or the Isle of Man.

It should also be noted that a double taxation agreement between the UK and your country of choice could result in your UK income falling outside the scope of UK tax but inside the scope of another country's tax regime. Double taxation agreements are considered in further detail later in the guide.

Before looking at living abroad in further detail, it is useful to remind ourselves of the general rules for income tax, capital gains tax and inheritance tax. The main points can be summarised as follows:

- Income tax is based primarily on residence. If you are resident in the UK, you are normally liable to UK tax on your worldwide income. If you are not resident you could still be liable to UK tax on income arising in the UK, but your non-UK income is outside the scope of UK income tax.

- Capital gains tax depends on both residence and ordinary residence. If you cease to be resident in the UK without also ceasing to be ordinarily resident here, you will remain liable to UK capital gains tax in respect of gains on your worldwide assets. If you cease to be both resident and ordinarily resident, you are outside the scope of UK capital gains tax, even on UK assets, subject to some anti-avoidance rules which we'll look at shortly.

- Inheritance tax is based on domicile. If a person is domiciled in the UK he is liable to UK inheritance tax on his worldwide assets even though he may be both resident and ordinarily resident in another country. If a person is not domiciled here, he is generally liable to inheritance tax on his UK assets only. (The deemed domicile rules outlined earlier should, however, be considered.)

Example 1

Brian is UK resident, ordinarily resident and domiciled during the 2006/2007 tax year. He will be liable to UK income tax on his worldwide income, UK capital gains tax on his worldwide gains and UK inheritance tax on his worldwide estate.

Example 2

Peter is UK non-resident and UK non-domiciled. He will still be liable to UK income tax on his UK income, although his overseas income will be outside the scope of UK income tax. On the assumption that he will remain non-resident for at least five complete tax years (see Chapter 5 on capital gains tax), Peter will not be liable to UK capital gains tax on either his UK or overseas gains. As he is non-UK domiciled he will be liable to UK inheritance tax on his UK estate – his overseas assets will be outside the scope of UK inheritance tax.

Example 3

David is UK non-resident but UK domiciled. He will be liable to UK income tax on any UK source income, exempt from UK capital gains tax on any gains yet he will still be liable for UK inheritance tax on his worldwide estate.

3.2 CONVINCING THE TAXMAN YOU ARE NON-RESIDENT

Chapter 2 outlined HM Revenue and Customs' rules regarding residence and domicile. While it is vital to understand the basic principles, what most people want to know is how they can become non-resident and reduce their exposure to UK taxes. We will look here at the practical steps that should be taken to help strengthen a claim for non-residence (domicile issues are looked at in detail later).

Selling Your Home

You should consider selling your UK house before leaving the country, assuming that any gain is covered by the Principal Private Residence relief and therefore escapes capital gains tax. If you are unsure whether this relief applies, further advice should be taken.

If the house cannot be sold before departure, you should try not to return to the UK at all until after it has been disposed of and is no longer available for you to use. An alternative to selling the house is to let it. However, care needs to be taken with this – depending on the circumstances, the taxman could argue that keeping property in the UK casts doubt on your intention to leave the country permanently.

This is particularly dangerous where there is a short-term lease, for example under four years, as HMRC could then argue that possession would be obtained within three years of departure. In such circumstances it would be advisable to obtain any evidence that the short-term let was made for commercial reasons and that you intend to be overseas for at least four years.

As stated previously, the taxman could look to see if you have an 'ongoing connection' with the UK to see if the UK is still really your home. If it is, Revenue could class you as still UK resident. Therefore anything you can do to support the fact that you have a new home overseas (such as selling UK property and limiting UK visits) would be helpful.

Returning to the UK

You should try to not return to the UK at any time between your departure and the next April 5th – in other words, during the tax year of departure. If you do, HMRC is unlikely to accept that you have left the country permanently until after the last such visit.

You should also try not to return to the UK at any time during the tax year following that in which you emigrate. It would then be unlikely that HMRC could class you as UK resident.

This is important as it shows a firm intention to break with this country and avoids you being classed as having an ongoing connection with the UK. If you wish to visit the UK during your first full tax year abroad it would not be fatal to your emigration claim, but any visits should be as few as possible and for short periods.

If you were to visit for up to three months (as you are theoretically able to do without being classified as UK resident under the 90-day test) this is likely to cast doubt on whether you really intended to live permanently abroad.

HMRC appears to be looking in detail at the position of individuals who claim non-resident status but actually live here for part of the year. They could also argue that you should be regarded as UK *ordinarily resident* and subject to UK capital gains tax on disposals of your worldwide assets.

It is also wise to keep a record of the reasons for the visits to the UK as these can demonstrate that any visits were unconnected with your 'ongoing lifestyle'.

The emigrant should also try to limit visits to the UK in the next two years. Visits during the part year of departure and the three tax years following departure are what will primarily influence the taxman's views on your residence status. If such visits are minimal there are unlikely to be problems.

Buying a Property Abroad

You should buy or rent a property in another country as soon as possible. This will have an impact on your ordinary residence status as it will show a permanent intention to move abroad. This is probably the single most important action you can take in persuading HMRC that you are not UK resident.

Many of the above steps are also useful when considering the emigrant's domicile.

3.3   HOW TO AVOID TIMING TRAPS

Strictly, the decision as to whether you are resident/ordinarily resident needs to be made for an entire tax year. In other words, you are not normally resident for part of a tax year.

Example 1

Keith is present in the UK from 6 April 2006 to 7 October 2006 (185 days). He would be resident in the UK for the entire 2006/2007 tax year.

In practice, an exception is made to this rule where a person leaves the UK to take up a 'permanent' residence elsewhere. Such a person is regarded as resident in the UK from 6 April to the date of his departure. In other words, rather than being regarded as UK resident for the whole of the tax year, the individual will be regarded as non-resident for the period that he is overseas.

This treatment is known as 'split year' treatment and is allowed by way of a Revenue and Customs concession. It should be noted that because this is a concession, if large amounts of tax are at stake, it may be unwise to rely too heavily on it.

Example 2

John left the UK permanently on 1 April 2007. He received a large overseas dividend on 3 April 2007. From a strict legal perspective, John would be UK resident for the whole of the 2006/2007 tax year and therefore the dividend would be subject to UK income tax.

However, as John has left the UK permanently (and has evidence to support this) the split year treatment would treat John as non-resident for the period 1 April to 5 April and therefore no UK income tax would be due on the overseas income.

In practice, as HMRC is entitled to refuse the benefit of the concession and could tax the dividend, it would be beneficial if possible to arrange for the dividend to be paid in the following tax year, in other words, from 6 April 2007.

The split year treatment is unlikely to be applied for capital gains tax purposes, unless the individual has been UK resident and ordinarily resident for less than four years.

3.4 HOW THE TAXMAN DECIDES RESIDENCE STATUS

When you leave the country you will provisionally be treated as ceasing to be resident and ordinarily resident in the UK from the day of departure – provided you can produce evidence to show that you intend to live permanently abroad for at least three years.

What can be regarded as acceptable evidence clearly depends on the particular facts. If you sell your UK property and purchase a new overseas property, this is suggestive of an intention to live permanently overseas. By contrast, if the UK property remains furnished and unlet, this could be regarded as evidence that you have not decided to make a permanent move.

If you cannot produce evidence at the date of departure, Revenue and Customs will normally treat you as remaining UK resident and ordinarily resident. After a period of three years they will review your position in order to make a final decision on whether you ceased to be resident and ordinarily resident in the UK at the date of departure.

They will look closely at the length of any visits to the UK and therefore, even though you may have intended to emigrate permanently, if something subsequently happened to persuade you to resume UK residence, it would be very difficult to persuade the tax authorities that you originally left the UK with the intention of emigrating permanently.

HMRC's approach is to consider an individual's residence/domicile position as part of the tax return. Your claim will therefore either be accepted or looked into further, as with any other entry on your return.

Before you submit your tax return it is possible to obtain an informal review of your status by submitting a form P85 (www.hmrc.gov.uk/cnr/p85.pdf) stating that you regard yourself as non-resident from a certain date.

Similarly if you are returning to the UK to live after being non-UK resident, you would complete a form P86 to inform HMRC of your return to UK residence (www.hmrc.gov.uk/cnr/P86.pdf).

HMRC will then have the opportunity to respond with a request for further information. It should be noted that Revenue and Customs is not legally bound under this procedure, although in practice they would be unlikely to enquire into your non-residency if they have previously agreed that you are non-resident – provided full information was initially provided. This therefore shows the importance of disclosing all relevant information to the taxman.

Chapter 4

How to Avoid UK Income Tax

4.1   INTRODUCTION

The basic rule is that UK residents are taxed on their worldwide income. Non-residents are only taxed on their UK income.

A person leaving the country to avoid income tax needs to remember that the UK, like most countries, claims the right to tax income arising in the UK, irrespective of whether it is earned by a resident or a non-resident.

You also need to take account of double tax treaties. A double tax treaty is an agreement between two countries that determines which country can tax which income, where an individual is a resident of both countries. The rules laid out in these treaties override the domestic tax legislation.

Most double taxation agreements provide for a substantial degree of exemption from UK tax for residents of treaty countries. This means the income is not taxed in the UK but is taxed in the other country. The drawback with this set-up is that most treaties are with countries with tax systems similar to our own – there are very few treaties with tax havens. Double tax treaties are discussed in more detail later in the guide.

So what can you do to minimise your UK income tax bill?

One solution is to dispose of all assets that generate UK income. Such a disposal would also provide evidence of your intention to move abroad permanently and would help to demonstrate that you are not UK ordinarily resident. Of course, the capital gains tax consequences of selling your assets would also have to be considered (see Chapter 5, How to Avoid UK Capital Gains Tax).

If selling your assets is not viable, it is worth noting that, apart from rental income, **most UK investment income received by non-residents is not liable to additional tax beyond what is deducted at source.** Let's take a closer look at the tax treatment of different types of income:

4.2   RENTAL INCOME

Non-residents have to pay tax on rental income from UK properties. There is a 22% withholding tax on the rent. If a firm of letting agents looks after your property, they are responsible for paying the withheld income tax to Revenue and Customs. Where there is no letting agent, it is the responsibility of the tenant. The letting agent/tenant has to account for this basic rate tax each quarter.

Where a tenant's gross rent is less than £100 per week, there is no requirement to deduct tax unless instructed to do so by HMRC.

Any tax withheld is allowed as a credit against your eventual UK tax liability calculated on your self assessment tax return.

Non-residents can also obtain permission to self assess any UK tax liability. This option avoids the withholding tax and is applied for by using form NRL1 (www.hmrc.gov.uk/cnr/nrl1_bw.pdf). Separate forms must be submitted for jointly held properties.

HMRC will generally give its approval provided:

- Your tax affairs are up to date, or
- You do not expect to be liable for any UK tax, or
- You have never had any UK tax obligations.

The tax on the profits of the rental business is then calculated on the self assessment tax return, with any income tax liability usually payable by the 31st January following the end of the tax year.

It is still possible to obtain a deduction for qualifying loan interest as long as it has been incurred 'wholly and exclusively' in relation to the rental income.

4.3   INTEREST & ROYALTIES

Interest and royalties paid overseas from the UK are subject to a 20% or 22% withholding tax, with no further liability – **in other words, no higher rate tax is payable.**

If you are not ordinarily resident in the UK you can apply to have your interest paid without any tax deducted, by completing a 'not ordinarily resident' declaration (www.hmrc.gov.uk/pdfs/r105.pdf). It should be noted that the interest is still subject to UK tax and would have to be accounted for in the annual tax return.

It may be worthwhile considering whether to transfer any cash in a UK bank account to an overseas account.

There would be no capital gains tax implications (as cash is not a chargeable asset for capital gains tax purposes) and no UK tax would be payable on your interest, provided you are non-resident.

And what about ISAs? Individuals can only make payments into Individual Savings Accounts (ISAs) if they are UK resident and ordinarily resident. So, for example, an individual who works abroad for a complete tax year and is regarded as non-resident will not be able to make ISA contributions during the period of non-residency. However, it's worth holding on to your existing ISAs as you will continue to enjoy the tax benefits no matter how long you live abroad.

There is also a special rule for investments in Government bonds (also known as gilts). Interest from these investments is completely tax free if you are non-resident.

Note that companies have beneficial treatment as a UK company could either make interest and royalty payments to another EU company free of UK withholding tax or claim a repayment of UK tax withheld due to the EU Interest and Royalties Directive. Similarly a UK company receiving interest and royalties from another EU company could receive these free of tax or reclaim the tax withheld thanks to the directive.

4.4   DIVIDENDS

There is no withholding tax on dividends, and for UK tax purposes, there will be no higher rate income tax charge. All dividends are treated as having been subject to a 10% tax charge at source and for non-UK residents, this will satisfy any basic rate income tax liability, so effectively dividend income is tax free in your hands.

Just as for UK residents, the 10% 'deemed' tax credit cannot give rise to a repayment of income tax.

However, depending on the terms of any double taxation agreement, income tax may STILL be payable in the home country.

4.5   PENSION INCOME

The general rules applying to investment income also apply to pension income.

A UK resident/ordinarily resident and domiciled individual is subject to UK income tax on UK and overseas pensions. However there is one key tax relief. A 10% deduction is given against certain overseas pension receipts. This means that such an individual is only taxed on 90% of his or her pension income.

If the pensioner is non-domiciled and is using the remittance basis to account for overseas income, then the 10% deduction will not be available.

Such a pensioner is fully liable to UK tax on UK pensions but overseas pensions will only be taxed when remitted to the UK, and the 10% deduction is not available.

If you are non-UK resident you will not pay UK tax on any overseas pensions.

If you are a UK expat pensioner who is receiving a UK pension you would usually be subject to UK income tax on your UK pension.

However, this is where double tax treaties could come to the rescue. Certain double tax treaties allow UK tax to be avoided and instead allow only the overseas country to levy tax. For example, the UK-Cyprus treaty grants sole taxing rights over UK pensions to Cyprus. The beauty of this is that Cyprus offers a pension income tax rate of just 5%! This may explain why Cyprus is becoming a popular destination for those wishing to retire abroad.

4.6   EMPLOYMENT INCOME

Employment income will be taxed differently depending on the residence/domicile status of the employee and where the duties are actually performed. There are three different circumstances under which employment income could be taxed. I'll call these the three 'cases':

Case I

This applies to individuals who are UK resident and ordinarily resident and covers both UK and foreign work duties.

The tax charge is on a receipts basis and the full amount of worldwide emoluments/salary is subject to UK income tax, except for one specific situation that falls within Case III (below).

Case II

This applies to non-resident individuals, or individuals resident but not ordinarily resident in the UK and covers only salary arising from UK duties.

Case III

This applies where an employee is either

- Resident but not ordinarily resident in the UK or

- The employee is UK resident/ordinarily resident but is of foreign domicile, works for a foreign employer and performs all duties outside of the UK.

In either of these cases the overseas salary can be assessed on a remittance basis, and is only subject to UK income tax when received in the UK.

Examples

David, of Jamaican domicile, has been working in the UK for a computer company. He is UK resident and will be fully taxed on his employment income under Case I.

Robert is a non-resident, yet he earns a salary from being a director of a UK company and pays regular visits to the UK head office throughout the year (but stays within the 90-day limit). He will be subject to income tax on his UK employment income under Case II. As he is non-resident, any overseas income will be exempt from UK income tax.

Peter, UK resident but non-UK domiciled, is to work overseas for four months for an overseas subsidiary of his UK employer.

The duties of the employment will be performed wholly abroad. He will be taxed on his overseas employment income under Case III on a remittance basis – in other words, he is subject to UK tax on income that is brought into the UK.

It is therefore important to understand the definition of UK and overseas duties.

A non-UK resident individual is not subject to UK income tax on salary received for duties performed wholly abroad. Any 'incidental duties' performed in the UK will not create a problem, provided these duties are clearly ancillary or subordinate to the overseas employment, for example going back to the UK for meetings at head office.

Example

Freddy has been offered a secondment to the Paris office of his employer. It is proposed that this is from 4 April 2006 to 3 April 2008. Freddy is happy with this as he is likely to be regarded as non-resident and not ordinarily resident from the date of his departure. (If you go abroad under a full-time contract of employment you will usually be regarded as non-resident and not ordinarily resident from the date of departure – see Chapter 8.)

Freddy must then look at the duties that he will be undertaking, as it is the earnings from the overseas employment that are exempt from UK income tax. Let's assume Freddy's job is to source French products that may be in demand from the British market. If as part of his role he is to return to the UK on a monthly basis and produce and advise on the production and marketing of these products, it may be that these duties are not incidental to the overseas employment, particularly if he is to spend, say, one week each month in the UK advising on this. If HMRC successfully argued the case, the employment income would need to be apportioned between UK and overseas income, with the UK income subject to UK income tax.

An emigrant who remains a Commonwealth citizen is entitled to claim the UK personal allowance, which is £5,035 for the 2006/07 tax year. You may, however, prefer not to make a claim for this allowance. Any claim made is usually dealt with by the Centre for Non Residents, which could reconsider on an annual basis whether or not you are UK resident. This could therefore be costly in terms of your time.

It's important to note that if you have any UK income which is normally taxed as a non-resident (such as UK rental income), you would not be able to make use of your tax-free personal allowance if you are also avoiding tax on your interest and dividends.

UK dividends and interest can usually be received by a non-UK resident free of UK tax. This is because something called S128 FA1995 (now contained in Chapter 3, Part 4 of the new Income Tax Act) applies to dividend and interest income and restricts the UK income tax to the tax deducted at source (if any), *provided no UK personal allowance is being claimed.*

Given that interest and dividends can be paid with no tax deducted there should be no UK tax charge on them but any rental income could not then be offset by the personal allowance.

4.7   UK NATIONAL INSURANCE

This is a tremendously complex area. However, generally no national insurance contributions are required to be paid by an individual who ceases to be ordinarily resident for social security purposes and who is paid by an overseas employer.

Where an individual is seconded abroad, Class 1 contributions are normally payable for 12 months after departure.

4.8 PENSION PLANNING

We take a closer look at working abroad later on. However, where an individual goes to work overseas there are a few issues to bear in mind as regards pensions:

- Will any benefits already accrued in a UK scheme be capable of being transferred into an overseas scheme?

- If you remain a member of a UK scheme, will any employer and employee contributions be taxed/tax deductible?

An individual sent overseas for a long period of service may wish to join a pension fund established in the overseas country.

The pension regime has undergone significant changes as from April 6 2006. One of the key differences is that it is possible to transfer benefits from an existing UK pension scheme to any overseas scheme free of UK tax, provided the overseas scheme is approved by the tax authorities as a Qualifying Recognised Overseas Pension Scheme (QROPS).

If the pension scheme is not a QROPS, any transfer could be subject to a 40% UK tax charge.

Alternatively, an employee may go abroad to work for a UK resident employer, and may decide to retain his UK occupational pension scheme. Again this has been significantly changed by the 2006 pension changes as both UK residents and non-UK residents can now be a member of a UK pension scheme. Therefore you could keep your UK scheme if you went to work overseas. Note that the application of the new pension rules to overseas transfers can be complex and you should take advice from a pensions specialist.

Example

Patrick has been offered an opportunity to work in his UK employer's Milan subsidiary for two years. He has been paying into the employer's occupational pension scheme and wishes to continue doing so.

As the employment is expected to last for two years and the overseas employer is part of the UK group, any pension contributions made by Patrick to his UK occupational scheme will be tax deductible.

4.9   OUT OF THE FRYING PAN INTO THE FIRE

A key problem is that most countries tax individuals on their worldwide income. On obtaining Spanish residence, for example, you would become liable to Spanish income tax on your worldwide income. With Spanish tax rates of up to 48%, avoiding UK tax is not as big a benefit as it seems!

However, not all countries tax residents on their worldwide income. In Malta, for example, individuals who are of non-Maltese domicile, and who are resident but not ordinarily resident in Malta, pay tax only on income arising in Malta, or income remitted there and this could be at rates as low as 15%. Similarly many of the well known tax havens such as the Bahamas, the Cayman Islands and Monaco don't levy any income taxes at all.

If you seek to minimise income tax, your choice of country of residence is critical. In addition, the terms of any applicable double tax treaty should be examined carefully. Double tax treaties are covered later in the book but it is worthwhile noting that you would be entitled to a 'set off' where tax was suffered in two countries on the same income.

Chapter 5

How to Avoid UK Capital Gains Tax

5.1 INTRODUCTION

In order for an individual to avoid capital gains tax it is usually necessary to remain non-resident for **five complete tax years**. Any gains on assets disposed of during the period of non-residence will then escape UK capital gains tax completely.

It should be noted that this rule only applies if you have been UK resident for at least four of the seven tax years prior to the year of your departure.

If you have not been UK resident for this time, it is still possible to avoid capital gains tax by becoming non-UK resident and non-UK ordinarily resident for the tax year of the disposal (for example, by working abroad under a full-time contract of employment that spans a complete tax year).

If you are subject to the five-year non-residence period and become UK resident within the five-year period, any gains on assets disposed of during your absence from the UK will be assessed as having arisen in the tax year in which they are sold.

5.2 COUNTRIES WITH GENEROUS CGT RULES

It should be noted that the above five-year rule for capital gains tax applies irrespective of what any double tax treaty says. However, you can use double tax treaties to potentially prevent a tax charge *overseas*.

The UK has concluded tax treaties with over 100 states and most of these give the country of residence sole taxing rights over capital gains (except if the gain arises from land or assets used in a permanent establishment, for example your home).

Therefore you can avoid UK capital gains tax if you move to a country with which the UK has concluded an appropriate double tax treaty. But you may still end up paying tax on your capital gains in the new country.

The key here is to find a treaty country that does not tax capital gains or has a favourable capital gains tax regime. For example, some countries such as South Africa and Australia will rebase the cost of your assets to their current market value and only tax you on gains generated thereafter.

The tax saving potential of this 'immigration at market value' rule should not be underestimated. Essentially it wipes out any existing gain on the asset for tax purposes. Capital gains are generally calculated by subtracting cost from selling price. So the higher the cost (by rebasing to current market value) the lower the capital gain and hence the lower your tax bill.

Example 1

Gerard, a UK resident individual, has built a big investment property portfolio in the UK. The estimated gain after all available reliefs is £800,000. This will result in capital gains tax of about £320,000. If Gerard emigrates to a country with the immigration at market value rule, the cost of the assets would now be their market value. Assuming he plans to stay in this country for at least five complete UK tax years, any sale would not be subject to UK capital gains tax. Any taxation charge in the country of residence would be minimal assuming property prices have not increased rapidly since emigrating. Gerard could therefore save significant amounts of capital gains tax, although the personal upheaval may outweigh the tax benefits.

Other countries also offer attractive tax benefits that are worth considering.

For example, the tax legislation in Canada allows an immigrant to shelter overseas income and capital gains for up to five years after arriving in the country. Maximum benefit can be made of this tax break by transferring income-producing assets that are situated outside Canada into an offshore trust.

All income and capital gains earned by these assets escape Canadian tax during the five-year period. If the trust continues in place after this and the person remains resident in Canada, the trust itself will become a Canadian resident and then be subject to Canadian tax on its worldwide income.

This would therefore allow non-Canadian assets to be protected from Canadian tax for a period of at least five years on taking up Canadian residence. You could then decide whether you wanted to continue to be a Canadian resident or whether the assets should be sold.

Note that if you were to become a Canadian citizen within the five-year period and then leave Canada, any income and capital gains produced by the offshore trust would be completely free of Canadian tax.

The advantage of using the offshore trust to hold the non-Canadian assets is that if you decided to remain resident in Canada as a Canadian resident and citizen beyond the five-year period, you could re-acquire the assets from the offshore trust at their current market value – for appreciating assets this would ensure a tax-free uplift in the base cost!

International Capital Gains Tax Rates

To give you an idea of how other countries tax capital gains, the table on the next page shows a selection of countries and the CGT rates that would generally apply to gains on assets that have been held for at least 12 months.

International Capital Gains Tax Rates	
	%
Australia	48.5
Belgium	0
Canada	23.5
China	20
France	26
Germany	0
Hong Kong	0
Italy	12.5 or 27
Japan	20
Mexico	0
Netherlands	0
Poland	0
Singapore	0
Sweden	30
United States	15

However, these are only a simple guide. Taking Australia, for instance, one method to reduce this rate would be to hold on to any asset for at least 12 months. If you do, you would only have to pay capital gains tax on half the gain you've made, which gives a taxpayer paying tax at the top tax rate an effective CGT rate of 24.25%. There are also often separate rates for gains on property, shares or other assets.

Some countries, such as Belgium and New Zealand do not have capital gains tax. However, certain gains are taxed as income.

Therefore, as always there is no substitute for obtaining good, up-to-date professional advice.

5.3 EXCEPTIONS TO THE FIVE-YEAR RULE

There are some exceptions to the 'five-year rule' that should be borne in mind:

- It only applies to individuals who go overseas after March 17th 1998. For those who were non-resident prior to this date it is only necessary that they are non-UK resident during the tax year the asset is sold in order for any gains to be tax free. Of course, in practical terms this rule was of most importance in the past, as most individuals who were non-resident on March 17th 1998, would now have been non-resident for five tax years – in other words their gains will be tax free.

- The rule only applies to assets held by the emigrant at the date of departure from the UK. Assets purchased during a tax year of non-residence are not subject to UK capital gains tax, provided you are also non-resident during the tax year they are sold. The requirement for five complete years of non-residence does not come into play in these circumstances.

Example

Peter left the UK in May 2003 and has not returned to the UK since this date. He bought a UK property in September 2004. HMRC accepted that Peter had been non-resident and not ordinarily resident since the date of his departure. If the property is sold in the 2005/2006 tax year it would be exempt from UK capital gains tax, as the property was both acquired and disposed of whilst Peter was a non-resident. Even if he was to subsequently become UK resident in the 2006/2007 tax year, the gain would not be taxable.

Therefore those thinking about investing in property prior to moving overseas could be better off delaying the acquisition until after the move overseas. Provided you sell the property while you are still non-resident, you will pay no tax even if you become UK resident before the expiration of the five-year period.

Note that UK tax legislation is generally subject to the terms of any relevant double tax treaty. Before the 2005 Budget it was possible to avoid the five-year rule by becoming resident in certain countries (for example, Belgium and Portugal to avoid tax on shares and Greece to avoid tax on property). You would then only need to be non-resident during the tax year the asset is sold.

This is no longer the case and the UK tax authorities now reserve the right to tax you if you come back to the UK within five years, irrespective of what any double tax treaty may say.

5.4   TRAPS TO AVOID IN THE YEAR YOU DEPART

Gains accruing on a disposal of assets in the tax year of departure are subject to capital gains tax even though the disposal may only occur after you have left the UK. This is an important trap to avoid.

Example

Paul left the UK on 17 November 2006. It is his intention to remain overseas permanently. He is therefore likely to be given split year treatment and treated as non-resident from 18 November 2006 onwards. He owns a property that has previously been rented out and is keen to dispose of it as soon as possible.

A disposal prior to 5 April 2007 would result in him paying capital gains tax in the 2006/2007 tax year.

If Paul were to dispose of the property after 6 April 2007 (in other words, at the beginning of the next tax year) the gain would arise in a tax year that he was non-resident. Provided he stays non-resident until on or after 6 April 2012, any gain will be completely free of UK capital gains tax.

If Paul were to become UK resident in, say, the 2008/2009 tax year HMRC will claim the right to tax him and the gain will be treated as having arisen in the 2008/09 tax year.

5.5   OUT OF THE FRYING PAN AND INTO THE FIRE

You need to always look at the overseas tax regime, and how it will apply to both your future income and assets, and your current assets, held at the date of emigration.

We've already looked at situations where assets should be sold after departure to take advantage of the capital gains tax exemption for non-residents, and any uplift in cost to market value.

What about the reverse scenario? It should not always be assumed that UK capital gains tax will be higher than that of the other country.

In fact there are a number of situations where disposing of assets whilst UK resident would reduce the overall tax charge, including:

- Where a CGT exemption exists such as principal private residence relief (PPR). A disposal whilst UK resident would ensure there was no chargeable gain. However, leaving the disposal until you become non-UK resident could substantially increase the tax charge if the new country of residence is not as favourable. Whilst many countries operate a form of PPR relief, few will deem your last 36 months of ownership as tax free – the UK does!

- Where UK reliefs significantly reduce any gain. The key example here would be business asset taper relief. This can potentially eliminate 75% of any gain, resulting in a tax rate for a higher rate taxpayer of 10%. We've already mentioned the use of Belgium, but if proper tax planning advice was not followed and, for example, shares were disposed of and taxed as income, tax could be payable at rates of up to 50%. The taxpayer would then be much worse off than a disposal whilst UK resident.

- Where the overseas country taxes gains at a much higher rate than the UK. Although the UK rate of 40% seems high, when other reliefs such as the annual exemption and taper relief are taken into account, it may well be the case that many emigrants (to Spain, for example) could end up paying more in CGT than a disposal whilst UK resident.

5.6   POSTPONING DISPOSALS AND AVOIDING CGT

An emigrant avoids capital gains tax if a disposal is delayed until the tax year following departure.

Therefore if Paul in the above example needed to postpone the disposal until the 2006/2007 tax year, no contract should be entered into until after April 6 2006.

One key trap to watch out for is, with the exception of land, Revenue and Customs may contend that there has been an oral contract for disposal prior to emigration. The emigrant should ensure that this possibility is considered and that no evidence is available to support this contention.

There are usually two possible methods of postponing a disposal: using conditional contracts and using options.

Conditional Contracts

A disposal under a conditional contract only occurs when the condition is satisfied. A contract is only conditional if:

- The condition is satisfied prior to the contract being 'completed', and

- It is within neither party's direct power to bring it about.

A good example of a conditional contract is a contract that is subject to a third party consent, for example the granting of planning permission.

Options

Options can be either call options, whereby the purchaser is entitled to call on the vendor to sell the asset, or put options in terms of which the vendor can require the purchaser to buy the asset. Options can therefore be used to delay the actual contract date, as the contract is not concluded until the option is satisfied.

5.7   AVOIDING CGT ON BUSINESS ASSETS

There is one key exception to the general rule that emigration takes UK assets out of the UK capital gains tax net, namely where a 'branch or agency trade' exists.

A branch or agency trade can exist when any business is being run from the UK. Therefore someone who leaves the country and retains a business and appoints a manager to run it, may find that a branch or agency trade exists.

In addition, a branch/agency trade exists if the emigrant is a partner in a UK partnership with capital gains apportioned between the partners. In this case, gains on UK assets are subject to UK capital gains tax if they are used by either the branch or trade.

A problem therefore arises where an individual operates via an unincorporated business (for example, a sole trader business or partnership). Once the proprietor leaves the country, the business will usually become a branch or agency trade and gains on the business assets will accordingly remain subject to capital gains tax.

There are two common ways around this difficulty:

- Sell the business before you emigrate and reinvest the proceeds in the assets of a new business situated abroad. In these circumstances, roll over relief may be available and the gain arising on the business assets can be effectively rolled over and, as the emigrant remains non-resident, the gain would be completely sheltered.

- Transfer the business to a company prior to leaving the country. If the transfer includes all the assets of the business, the business is a trading business and shares in the company are the sole consideration received by the individual, then the capital gain is rolled over against the cost of the company shares. As the shares are not a business, there will be no branch/agency capital gains tax charge when you sell the shares.

Care must, however, be taken with the latter method, particularly given the large number of cases coming before the courts regarding anti-avoidance. To avoid attack under anti-avoidance principles, the transfer to the company should take place before the sale is negotiated.

5.8   SALE OF A FORMER HOME

An individual leaving the UK may decide to not dispose of a UK home until after they have left the UK. It should be remembered that there is no UK capital gains tax on the sale of a main residence. As a result, sale of such a property whilst UK resident is still a good option.

On becoming resident in another country, care must be taken as regards the tax liability in the new country of residence, as many countries charge residents capital gains tax on their worldwide disposals.

In such a case, it is necessary to identify whether the UK has a double tax treaty with the country in question as these treaties can determine which country has sole taxing rights. The problem in relation to property is that under the terms of most double tax treaties, 'immovable property' can be taxed in the country where the property is located (in other words, the UK) as well as taxed overseas.

Therefore although no UK liability would arise provided you satisfied the five-year test (in other words, you did not become UK resident within five tax years of the date of departure), the overseas country where you are now resident could potentially tax your gains.

Example

Catriana emigrated to Spain during the 2006/2007 tax year. She has purchased a property in Spain and has become a Spanish resident. She still owns a UK property, which has increased in value significantly. She has decided to sell the UK property and needs to know whether there will be any UK or Spanish tax on a disposal of the property.

Under the terms of Article 13(1) of the UK-Spain double tax treaty (see Appendix), the capital gain arising on the sale of the property can be liable to tax in the country where the property is situated. This is further developed by Article 24(4), which provides that the property will be treated as a UK source, and therefore liable to UK tax.

Since an individual who is neither resident nor ordinarily resident in the UK is exempt from UK capital gains tax (unless the assets are used in connection with a UK trade), the disposal would escape tax altogether in the UK. However the gain would need to be declared for Spanish tax purposes.

5.9   FAVOURABLE TAX JURISDICTIONS

There are a number of countries that offer favourable tax regimes. Given the complexities involved, and the differing approaches taken by other tax authorities, it is essential that you obtain detailed and specific advice from a suitably qualified tax specialist in the relevant country.

In addition, tax should not be your main consideration when considering a move abroad. Other factors that you should probably consider include political and economic stability, protection of property rights, guarantees against asset expropriation, the level of government regulation, investment concessions, currency restrictions, domestic crime levels, access to quality healthcare, climate, distance from the UK/family, communication and transportation, banking secrecy and ease of obtaining residence.

One of the biggest dangers facing those who move abroad but retain significant UK assets and income is currency movements. The Euro, for example, has gyrated wildly against the Pound since its launch and other currencies behave even more erratically. This can play havoc with your personal financial planning.

It's also critical to avoid substituting a lower tax bill for other financial burdens, such as expensive property and high living costs in your new country of residence.

Some of the countries that offer favourable tax regimes include:

The Cayman Islands

The Cayman Islands impose no taxes other than import duties and stamp duty. In addition, they have no double tax treaties.

Andorra

There are no taxes in Andorra. The only things you have to watch out for are rates and some property transaction taxes. There is no double tax treaty with the UK.

Gibraltar

The main benefit of Gibraltar is that there is no capital gains tax or VAT. Income tax is, however, payable. Individuals pay quite high taxes on their income in Gibraltar unless they can take advantage of 'High Net Worth Individual' status (also known as category 2 status), which is granted to certain wealthy individuals. Income tax is usually payable at rates of up to 45% but High Net Worth Individuals are assessed on only a fraction of their total taxable income.

Cyprus

Cyprus charges both income tax and capital gains tax, although capital gains tax does not apply to profits from the sale of overseas property by non-residents, or to the profits of residents who were non-resident when they purchased the asset. The capital gains tax rate is 20%.

Malta

Individuals who are domiciled and ordinarily resident in Malta pay income tax on their worldwide income. Individuals who are domiciled elsewhere, and who are resident but not ordinarily resident in Malta pay tax on their income arising in Malta, or remitted there, but not on capital gains.

Monaco

Monaco levies no personal taxes, although there are inheritance and gift taxes, along with business profits tax. VAT is also charged on goods and services.

5.10   USING ENTERPRISE INVESTMENT SCHEMES

A capital gains tax bill can be deferred by reinvesting in Enterprise Investment Scheme Shares. The ability to defer capital gains tax by reinvesting in venture capital trusts was scrapped from April 6 2004.

An important point to note is that any relief given to an individual on shares acquired by him (or in certain circumstances his spouse) may be clawed back if the individual ceases to be resident or ordinarily resident in the UK – unless for overseas employment on a short secondment.

Therefore any gains deferred under the Enterprise Investment Scheme will be brought back into the tax net.

Example

Jack sold his investment company and ended up with a taxable capital gain of £500,000. He reinvested this gain in qualifying Enterprise Investment Scheme shares in order to defer paying capital gains tax. He has purchased a property in Majorca and intends to regularly holiday in Spain. Jack needs to be very careful that he does not spend too much time abroad and become UK non-resident. If he does there could be severe consequences:

- *He will be non-resident, so still liable to UK income tax on any UK source income.*

- *He has no overseas income and so will not benefit from the exemption from UK income tax on overseas income.*

- *He will still be ordinarily resident and within the scope of UK capital gains tax.*

- *He will still be UK domiciled and therefore within the scope of UK inheritance tax.*

- *He will have a 'deemed gain' in relation to the gain held over in the tax year of departure (£500,000). Given that his cash is tied up in Enterprise Investment Scheme shares this could cause severe cash flow problems.*

5.11 OFFSHORE INVESTMENTS FOR UK RESIDENTS

What about the typical British person who is both UK resident and UK domiciled – are there any offshore techniques they can use to minimise UK tax?

The first point to bear in mind is that, as a UK resident, you will be taxed on your worldwide income and gains under domestic tax legislation. Therefore, the scope to generate returns in a more tax-efficient manner is limited.

Example

Herbert a UK resident and domiciled individual wants to invest in overseas equities. He decides to invest purely through an offshore broker, and will invest in shares quoted on the US stock market. He will be fully liable to UK capital gains tax on his profits.

However, there are specific exceptions contained within the tax legislation that apply to offshore bonds.

Offshore Bonds

Qualifying offshore bonds allow investors to 'roll up' their returns – this means tax is only paid at the end of the investment period (usually five to 10 years) when the investment is cashed in.

A withdrawal of up to 5% can be taken each year, with tax only payable at the end of the investment period. If you exceed the 5% limit a tax liability is triggered.

It is also possible to switch in and out of different investment funds within an offshore bond wrapper without these transfers being classified as chargeable events for capital gains tax purposes.

Investment in these qualifying offshore bonds can prove highly tax effective. Investments grow virtually tax free within the fund, benefiting from what is known as 'gross roll up'. This means that, rather than an investment being taxed on an ongoing basis, the funds grow without the encumbrance of tax.

Whilst there may be personal tax to pay when the investment is cashed in, proper tax planning, such as arranging your affairs so that you are non-UK resident at the date of encashment, can help reduce this.

Gross roll up can lead to dramatic increase in the amount of money invested.

For example, an individual investing £50,000 in a bond, assuming a 7% growth rate, would have the following amounts at the end of a 20-year period:

Onshore bond	£145,000
Offshore bond (taxed on encashment at 22%)	£161,000
Offshore bond – no income tax	£192,000

Therefore the offshore bond could accumulate approximately £47,000 of additional capital which could be used for retirement.

Capital gains tax is not levied within the fund on offshore bonds, so an investment may be actively managed focusing solely on the investment considerations rather than being subject, as in the UK, to capital gains tax within the fund.

Savings can often be made with offshore bonds since investors can buy and sell qualifying investments held within the bond without any liability to capital gains tax. Many offshore bond providers offer links to third-party, household name, investment companies, so finding a suitable investment shouldn't be difficult.

However, after the 2004 Budget, HMRC announced changes that will affect when offshore investment bonds will be able to benefit from the income tax and gross roll up treatment described above.

These changes are quite technical, and as such it would be advisable to seek confirmation from any potential fund provider whether the chosen fund falls within the above tax rules.

If the fund does not qualify for the gross roll up, the investment would be treated just as any other UK investment. This would eliminate the UK tax benefit as purchases and disposals of the investments or units within the bond would be subject to UK capital gains tax.

Overseas investments, and in particular the taxation of offshore bonds, is a complex area, and you should therefore take professional advice when considering your investment strategy.

Chapter 6

How to Avoid Inheritance Tax

6.1   INTRODUCTION

The general rule is that an individual domiciled in the UK will be subject to inheritance tax on his or her *worldwide assets*. Non-UK domiciled individuals are only subject to UK inheritance tax on their *UK assets*.

In order to lose your UK domicile you will need to build up evidence to show that you have abandoned your UK domicile of origin and have acquired a new domicile of choice. In layman's terms, this involves 'cutting your ties' with the UK and establishing a new permanent home overseas.

This is something that many who leave the country do not do... with disastrous tax consequences. Frequently they return to the UK on many occasions, keeping within the 90 days a year *income tax* limit. This pattern of behaviour is likely to indicate that you have not abandoned your domicile of origin, with the result that you will be subject to UK inheritance tax on your worldwide assets.

In order to safeguard your overseas estate from inheritance tax, you are likely to have to make some significant changes to your lifestyle in order to produce evidence that you have a new domicile of choice.

6.2   HOW TO LOSE YOUR UK DOMICILE

You should take as many of the following steps as possible in order to show evidence of an intention to acquire a new domicile of choice:

- Take up nationality in the new country.
- Join clubs and other social organisations in the new country.
- Dispose of UK investments.
- Resign from clubs in the UK.
- Close UK bank accounts.

- Buy an overseas burial plot.
- Avoid subscriptions to British newspapers.
- Dispose of all UK private residences.
- Buy a new residence in the new country.
- Make a will under the laws of the new country.
- Build up a new circle of friends in the new country.
- Avoid retaining directorships in the UK.
- Exercise any vote in the new country.

It should be noted that none of the above factors are in themselves conclusive. However, Revenue and Customs will look at all the factors that can be put in evidence to determine whether there is a real intention to reside permanently in the new country.

Obtaining a non-UK domicile of choice does not protect you completely from UK inheritance tax. You will still be liable to tax on your UK assets. If the value of these assets is less than the nil rate band (currently £285,000 for the 2006/2007 tax year) it is probably not worth taking any further action, unless you expect your assets to rise significantly in value.

If you wish to keep significant UK assets, one option would be to place an overseas company between yourself and your assets. What you would then own are shares in an overseas company – a non-UK asset. Care must, however, be taken with the disposal, to ensure that any gain falls outside of the scope of UK capital gains tax. The use of offshore companies is explained in detail later on.

6.3   HOW TO ESTABLISH AN OVERSEAS DOMICILE

In practical terms it is difficult for UK emigrants to convince the UK taxman that they have a non-UK domicile.

A form, 'DOM 1', is available from the HM Revenue and Customs website (www.hmrc.gov.uk/cnr/dom1.pdf) which can be used where an individual considers they are non-UK domiciled. However, it is only necessary for Revenue and Customs to consider your domicile if it is immediately relevant in deciding your UK income tax and/or capital gains tax liability. If you are non-resident, this will not be an issue, as you will not in any event be subject to UK capital gains tax or income tax on overseas capital gains and income.

Therefore, by ticking the non-domicile box in your tax return, or completing form DOM 1, HMRC is unlikely to enter into correspondence with you regarding your tax status, as your domicile will have no impact on your immediate UK income tax or capital gains tax liability. For a non-resident, the only impact of non-domicile status is for UK inheritance tax.

It cannot be assumed that you are of non-UK domicile if HMRC does not look into the issue during your lifetime. If you wish to determine your domicile position prior to death, there are methods available.

If you're non-UK domiciled and living in the UK, the simplest way to establish non-UK domicile status with the taxman is to ensure that you have a small amount of overseas income that is not fully remitted to the UK. You'd then usually enter this on your tax return and HMRC would need to look into your circumstances to decide whether you should be taxed on the full interest earned (like a UK domiciliary) or only on the interest actually brought into the UK.

The easiest way to achieve this is to ensure you place some funds in an overseas interest-bearing account and don't remit all the interest generated.

The other scenario is where a UK domiciliary emigrates and wants to establish an overseas domicile of choice.

Testing your domicile status in this case is more difficult, however one method would be to gift cash or assets (above the £285,000 nil rate band) to a discretionary trust or company. Provided the cash or assets are situated overseas, inheritance tax would be payable unless you have lost your UK domicile. Accordingly, if the taxman does not try and make you pay inheritance tax it will be clear that he accepts that you have acquired a foreign domicile.

6.4   RETAINING YOUR DOMICILE OF ORIGIN

Many UK immigrants and their children are non-UK domiciled. There are substantial tax advantages to be had from retaining this status. In particular:

- Overseas assets can be passed though the family free from UK inheritance tax.

- Overseas assets can be used to generate income offshore. Provided the income is not brought into the UK, there will be no liability to UK taxation.

- There are greater opportunities to use offshore trusts and companies, as many of the anti-avoidance rules apply only to UK domiciliaries.

As always, however, you and your family need to be careful:

Firstly, the deemed domicile rules (Chapter 2) will deem you to be UK domiciled for inheritance tax purposes, after you've been here for 17 years. Many families will find that their children are subject to UK inheritance tax as a result of this rule. Note, however, that the deemed domicile rule only applies for inheritance tax purposes. Your children could still accumulate assets offshore without paying any UK tax.

The next risk is that the taxman may contend that you or your children have acquired a UK domicile of choice. This is very likely if you have stayed in the UK for a number of years. To establish that you have acquired a UK domicile of choice, the evidence would need to point to the fact that you intend to stay in the UK permanently.

There are a number of other options that could be considered to minimise UK inheritance tax. These are considered elsewhere in the book, however they include:

- Using mortgages/loans to reduce the value of your estate.

- Using an offshore structure to avoid estate taxes.

- For non-domiciliaries, disposing of UK assets and purchasing assets overseas. The capital gains tax implications (both UK and overseas) should be considered, however, for an individual who intends to remain overseas for a significant period, UK CGT would not be an issue, and dependent on the terms of any double tax treaty and domestic tax legislation, there may not in fact be any overseas tax charged.

- Investment in assets that qualify for Business Property Relief (BPR), for example shares in unquoted trading companies and assets used in a trading business.

Chapter 7

The Advantages of Being Non-Domiciled

7.1   NON-UK DOMICILIARIES

Individuals who are UK resident/ordinarily resident but retain a foreign domicile enjoy preferential tax treatment in a number of respects.

The type of person who can exploit these tax breaks is typically someone who was born outside the UK but currently lives here. Their children are usually also able to take advantage of these tax-planning opportunities.

The main tax benefit is that overseas income and capital gains are only subject to UK income tax and capital gains tax on the 'remittance basis'. This means that tax is paid only when the funds are brought into the UK. This is a fantastic tax break because it means that your investments can grow tax free for many years and potentially indefinitely.

Inheritance tax, being based on domicile, would not normally apply to overseas assets. However, the deemed domicile rules for inheritance tax purposes will result in your worldwide estate being subject to inheritance tax if you are UK resident for 17 out of the last 20 years.

7.2   INCOME TAX PLANNING

A foreign domiciliary is subject to income tax on a remittance basis in respect of income arising from foreign securities and overseas possessions. For this purpose a trade carried on outside the UK is regarded as an overseas possession.

But what about salary?

Foreign Emoluments and Salary

These were considered earlier, however it is useful to explain the rule again. There is a separate rule for certain foreign emoluments (emoluments in this context can be taken to mean salary). A foreign domiciliary who is resident in the UK is taxed on a remittance basis only on any emoluments which are paid to him (a) by a non-UK resident employer and (b) in respect of an office or employment, the duties of which are only performed abroad.

If your work duties are not performed abroad only, then the income is taxed as and when it arises.

7.3 USING SPLIT CONTRACTS TO REDUCE INCOME TAX

It is not uncommon for foreign domiciliaries working in the UK to have two separate employments. One will cover the UK duties and the other will cover the overseas duties.

The benefit of this arrangement is that the overseas duties will only be subject to UK tax on the remittance basis (in other words, under Case III as mentioned in Chapter 4).

Clearly legal advice should be taken as to the precise provisions of the employment contracts, however it is worthwhile noting that care should be taken to ensure that a degree of 'commerciality' is retained.

Each contract should be reasonable (for example, the level of remuneration should be closely related to the duties to be performed) and should clearly lay out the employment duties. If possible, separate employers/companies should be used, so that the employment does not appear to have been artificially separated.

Example

Richard a non-UK domiciliary has been offered full time employment with his UK employer's Rome office. The duties of the employment will be split approximately 40% (UK), 60% (Rome).

On this basis, all of the income (assuming Richard is UK resident) would be subject to UK income tax under Case I (see Chapter 4). The remittance basis would not apply as the employment duties are not only performed abroad.

If separate contracts were used for the UK and Rome employment duties, then the UK employment would be subject to UK income tax, whereas the Rome employment would fall under the remittance basis.

However, it's important to note that HMRC issued a tax bulletin in April 2005 that covered the use of split contracts.

It states that split contracts will be examined in detail where:

- On the facts there is one single employment and the employment has been artificially separated, or

- Where duties of a more substantial nature have been performed in the UK, and you couldn't say that the UK duties were 'merely incidental' to the overseas employment (in which case they would have been ignored).

This more or less ties in with our previous view and when considering the use of split contracts you should pay particular care to the overall commerciality of the arrangement including the allocation of duties between the UK and overseas, the allocation of remuneration and whether there is, in reality, one employment.

7.4   CAPITAL GAINS TAX PLANNING

As stated above, capital gains in respect of assets situated outside of the UK are taxable on the remittance basis. Any capital losses are not allowable.

Example

Steve, a non-UK domiciliary has been living in the UK for eight years and is therefore classed as UK resident. He has overseas assets that originally cost him £100,000 and he is planning to sell them for £150,000.

The gain of £50,000 (less any reliefs) will not be subject to UK capital gains tax – provided the proceeds of £150,000 are not brought into the country, for example, deposited in a UK bank account or used to settle UK debts.

If only part of the proceeds is remitted, then only part of the gain is taxable. For example, if £15,000 of proceeds is remitted to the UK, £5,000 would be taxable. (Note how the proportions are what matter. £5,000 is to £15,000 what £50,000 is to £150,000.) One way of using the remittance basis to avoid paying tax is to remit just enough of the proceeds to make use of your annual capital gains tax exemption.

So if proceeds of £26,400 were remitted in the 2006/07 tax year, the taxable gain would be £8,800. As the annual capital gains tax exemption is £8,800, the gain would be completely tax free.

7.5 MAKING THE MOST OF THE REMITTANCE RULES

It is often advisable for foreign domiciliaries to have at least three overseas bank accounts:

- The first account for your existing capital.

- The second account to deposit the proceeds of any asset disposals.

- The third account to contain the interest from the first two accounts, along with any other foreign source income.

The point of this exercise is to segregate your foreign income and gains.

If you want to bring money into the country you should first remit funds from the first bank account. This can usually be done tax free. If further funds are required, then withdrawals can be made from the second account, which would effectively subject the withdrawals to capital gains tax. However, it is possible these amounts will be tax free if they are covered by the annual exemption of £8,800. Finally, withdrawals from the third account would be subject to income tax.

Another advantage of utilising these accounts is that, for inheritance tax purposes, the foreign bank accounts of a non-UK domiciliary will usually be outside the scope of UK inheritance tax.

Example

Hercule, who was born in Belgium, has been offered a contract of employment with a UK company. It is envisaged that he will be in the UK for five years before returning to Belgium.

Hercule has significant assets in France and has decided to dispose of his main residence before he commences his UK employment. Any proceeds of this sale should be put into overseas account 1. One year after the commencement of his contract, he hears that the Belgian property market is about to collapse and he decides to sell his other Belgian property. The proceeds of this sale should go into overseas account 2. Any overseas income that he earns, for example rental income from his properties or interest on his overseas bank accounts should be deposited in overseas account 3.

Hercule may never need to use any of his foreign income/proceeds during his period of stay in the UK, in which case none of the foreign income/gains would be taxable. If he does require any funds they should be remitted in the following order:

- ***Account 1*** *– Not subject to UK capital gains tax as the assets were disposed of before Hercule was UK resident.*

- ***Account 2*** *– Subject to UK capital gains tax on a remittance basis, as the disposal occurred while Hercule was UK resident but non-domiciled. Capital gains tax is usually preferable to income tax as there are more reliefs available.*

- ***Account 3*** *– Subject to UK income tax on the remittance basis as overseas income of a UK resident/non-domiciliary.*

7.6   PAYING LESS TAX ON INVESTMENT INCOME

As UK resident non-domiciliaries are only subject to tax on the remittance basis it is often suggested that they should transfer their UK savings offshore and avoid UK income tax.

This is certainly possible. However, it is also clearly beneficial to keep existing overseas assets such as property and bank accounts and avoid bringing the money into the UK in the first place. This then avoids an extra 'layer' of UK tax.

Any cash saved by a UK resident will have already been subject to UK income tax, either as salary or business income. Transferring the cash into an overseas account does not result in any UK tax charge and any interest earned would be overseas income. This would be subject to UK income tax only if it was brought into the UK. If funds were required it would be beneficial to remit part of the cash deposited abroad as this is not overseas income, merely cash earned in the UK and credited to an overseas account.

This is easier to manage if a separate account is set up into which the interest is paid. It would then be clear that the cash remitted to the UK was not the overseas interest income.

Finally, it is important to note that the concept of 'remittance' can have a wide meaning. For example, using a UK credit card and clearing the balance with overseas income would constitute a remittance to the UK.

Using Overseas Loans

Another opportunity available for non-UK domiciliaries to avoid the remittance rules is to obtain an overseas loan (used, for example, to buy a UK property), with the interest on the loan paid out of offshore income. The payment of the overseas interest should not constitute a remittance and is in fact often used as a tax-efficient alternative to raising funds from a UK lender (where the payment of interest would clearly be a UK remittance).

It's worthwhile noting that the tax legislation specifically addresses the use of overseas loans and states that if any overseas income is used to pay a 'UK linked' debt, then the amount paid is taxed as a UK remittance. It defines a 'UK linked debt' as:

"... a) a debt for money lent to the person in the United Kingdom, or for interest on money so lent,

(b) a debt for money lent to the person outside the United Kingdom and received in the United Kingdom, or

(c) a debt incurred for satisfying-

> *(i) a debt falling within paragraph (a) or (b), or*

> *(ii) another debt falling within this paragraph...."*

It's important to realise that there is a difference between paying off the principal or capital element of a loan, and just paying off the interest.

Let's say you take out a loan overseas, which you use to fund UK expenditure, and use overseas income to repay part of the *capital* element of the loan. In this case a non-domiciled taxpayer will be treated as having remitted the income used to pay off the loan and that income will therefore be taxed.

But if you use overseas income to pay off just the *interest* on the loan, this should not be classed as a remittance of foreign income. This principle should apply even if you bring the borrowings into the UK.

There is a downside, however.

In the same way that bank interest usually has 20% income tax deducted at source, the same rule can apply to other types of interest as well.

The tax legislation is widely drafted and can require tax to be deducted by the payer (you) where the interest is from a UK *source* but the payment is made overseas.

Revenue and Customs would look at a number of factors to determine whether the interest has a UK source:

- The residence of the debtor (this is usually taken to be the place where the debt will be enforced),

- The source from which interest is paid,

- Where the interest is paid, and

- The nature and location of any security for the debt.

In order to ensure that the debt does not have a UK source and is not subject to the tax deduction provisions you should as a minimum ensure that:

- The borrower is not a UK resident.

- The loan is not secured on the UK property.

- The interest is actually paid outside the UK and from overseas income.

Alternatively, you could use the capital account procedures mentioned previously to separate your capital from your income and ensure that what is brought into the UK is not a remittance of income.

Cessation of Source

Non-UK domiciliaries frequently own offshore investments that generate overseas interest.

Because they are non-UK domiciled they are only subject to UK income tax if the income is brought back to the UK.

One way such individuals may be able to remit income tax-free is to rely on the 'cessation of source' rule.

This rule relies on the well established principle that income can't be taxed in a tax year, unless the source from which it is derived also exists during the tax year.

Effectively this means that you should be able to remit income such as bank interest free of tax if you close an account in one tax year and then remit the accumulated income in the next tax year (because there is no longer an income source that can be charged to tax).

Revenue and Customs has traditionally accepted that a remittance is not taxable if it is from a source that has ceased prior to the tax year concerned.

HMRC's own internal manuals state:

"Where, however the source of the income has ceased before the commencement of the year in which a remittance is made such income should be excluded from the computation of liability."

So closing a bank account in one tax year and transferring funds to another bank account the following tax year should help you get around the remittance rules.

Note that to protect your position you should undoubtedly use different banks or at the very least use accounts that are substantially different (for example, transfer your funds from a deposit account to a current account) to ensure that the second account really is a totally separate source.

Gifts Abroad

Another popular way of avoiding the remittance provisions is to give overseas income away abroad with the recipient then bringing it back into the UK.

As the non-domiciled person is not personally bringing the income into the UK he cannot be charged to UK tax. And the recipient is also not subject to tax because he has not earned any overseas income – instead he has received a gift overseas (which is not taxable).

So you could use this technique to transfer bank interest or other overseas income to a relative (for example, your spouse or adult child) or to a trust which would then transfer the cash to the UK.

Revenue and Customs has stated that it could challenge gifts abroad if either the gift was not completed abroad or if financial consideration for the 'gift' has been received in the UK. Therefore in terms of timing it is crucial that the gift actually takes place abroad and isn't transferred into a UK bank account.

If you want to rely on this exemption, you need to be careful to ensure that the gift overseas is not a sham. For example, if you gift the cash to your wife and she brings the income into the UK and buys you a new car with it, there is be a strong likelihood that HMRC could challenge this and seek to tax you on the income.

However, if your wife keeps the cash in a separate account and uses it to buy her own personal assets or to pay her own personal expenses it should be regarded as a 'genuine' gift.

All of these options for non-UK domiciliaries to remit income free of UK taxes are potentially complex and should be discussed in detail with your professional adviser.

7.7 INCORPORATING YOUR BUSINESS TO AVOID CAPITAL GAINS TAX

We have already mentioned that one of the options open to a possible emigrant who owns a UK business is to incorporate the business and dispose of the shares whilst non-resident. Suppose the individual is of non-UK domicile and cannot become non-resident at the date of disposal and for five complete tax years.

Could he incorporate his business (using an overseas company) and then have any disposal taxed on the remittance basis? This question is best answered by means of an example:

Example

John is of French domicile, yet has been resident in the UK for five years. During this period he has built up a successful publishing business. He now wishes to retire to France and is interested in minimising his UK tax liabilities.

In theory, it would be possible for John to transfer his business to a non-resident company (with no immediate capital gains tax charge).

He would have then converted a UK asset (in other words, the trade and assets) into an overseas asset (the company shares). Any subsequent gain on disposal of the shares would be assessed on a remittance basis, and provided the proceeds were retained overseas, there should be no liability to pay UK capital gains tax.

This is, of course, not a straightforward course of action and there would be a number of anti-avoidance provisions that would need to be considered. Therefore any individual considering such a course of action should undoubtedly take professional advice as the taxman can and has successfully challenged this technique, particularly where there has been no commercial motive for transferring the trade to an overseas company, and where the transfer was made in anticipation of a sale.

7.8   BUYING PROPERTY OVERSEAS

For those who are UK resident and ordinarily resident but non-UK domiciled, purchasing overseas property can offer a number of attractive tax breaks. For income tax and capital gains tax purposes the remittance basis applies. This means that any rental income obtained from the overseas property will be exempt from UK tax, provided the income is not remitted to the UK.

In addition, when the property is eventually sold, no UK capital gains tax will be payable unless the funds are brought into the country.

However, the benefit of the remittance basis is for many more apparent than real. Overseas tax is likely to be payable, unless the property is purchased in a tax haven of some kind. Most double tax treaties state that immovable property can be taxed in the country in which it is located (in other words, the overseas jurisdiction) as well as the owner's country of residence. Therefore for a non-UK domiciliary investing in overseas property it is overseas tax that will have the biggest impact. And the European countries most individuals have traditionally invested in tend to have high tax rates.

For example, in Spain sales of property by non-Spanish residents are taxed at 35% (although the European Commission is referring this to the European court of Justice on the grounds that it is discriminatory, given that the tax rate for Spanish residents can be as low as 15%).

The gain is calculated as the difference between the sales price and the original purchase price, including any investment made or improvement work carried out. There is also an adjustment to take account of inflation. In addition, the purchaser must retain 5% of the price and pay this as tax on behalf of the non-resident.

The non-UK domiciled UK resident investing in Spain will also need to pay any local taxes relating to the property, as well as other domestic taxes. For example, Spain has a wealth tax, which would tax the value of a non-resident's Spanish assets above a certain amount.

In Italy, capital gains realised on the sale of property are subject to personal income tax. This tax is calculated on the taxpayer's total income. A progressive rate is used and the tax is settled by means of an annual income statement. The rate can be as high as 33%, however the gain is completely exempt if the property is owned for at least five years.

The gain is calculated as the difference between the amount received and the original purchase cost of the property. Capital gains realised on the sale of building land are also subject to income tax, irrespective of the period of ownership.

There are also other exemptions. For example, gains arising on the sale of inherited property or your main residence are not subject to Italian tax.

In France, as a non-resident, the UK resident non-domiciliary pays capital gains tax on the gain arising on the disposal of French property. This is usually deducted from the sale proceeds by the 'Notaire' who pays it over to the local tax authorities. At present, EU residents pay capital gains tax at the rate of 16%.

It is possible to deduct costs such as original purchase costs (notaire's fee, estate agent's fee), and the cost of renovation work (but not simple redecorating costs), provided that these haven't also been offset against any rental income.

The amount of the taxable gain is then subject to taper relief if it has been owned for more than five years. For each year that the property has been held beyond this initial five-year period, the gain is reduced by 10% (for ten years of ownership, the reduction is thus 50%). Therefore, if a property has been owned for more than 15 years, the relief is 100% and no capital gains tax is payable.

Just as in the UK, there are a number of exclusions and exemptions, and if you are considering purchasing a property in any overseas jurisdiction, it is essential to obtain tax advice from a tax specialist in the country in question.

The only sure-fire way for a non-domiciliary to avoid capital gains tax altogether is to purchase overseas property in a country that:

- Levies no capital gains tax, for example the Isle of Man.

- Levies no taxes at all, for example a tax haven such as Monaco or the Bahamas.

- Has specific exemptions to exclude any gain from a tax charge (for example, Italy or France).

Inheritance Tax

Again, from a UK tax perspective, there would be no UK inheritance tax impact. As a non-UK domiciliary, your taxable estate would include only your UK assets. However, overseas tax would be payable, unless the property was located in a country that did not levy inheritance tax.

Use of Trusts

As a non-UK domiciliary, an offshore trust could be created. For inheritance tax purposes, the trust would not be subject to UK IHT as the assets of the trust would be overseas assets.

From a capital gains tax perspective, the trustees should not be liable to UK capital gains tax, as the trust would be non-resident. Provided the settlor retains his non-UK domicile status, many of the UK anti-avoidance provisions attributing/deeming gains would not apply.

Provided the overseas jurisdiction did not levy capital gains tax, there would also be no overseas tax charge (for example in the Isle of Man).

Chapter 8

Working Overseas:
A Powerful Tax Shelter

8.1   INTRODUCTION

If you go abroad under a full-time contract of employment you will usually be regarded as non-resident and not ordinarily resident from the date of departure if:

- All your work duties are performed overseas, or any duties performed in the UK are incidental to the overseas employment, and

- Your absence from the UK is for a period which includes a complete tax year, and

- Visits to the UK do not exceed six months or more in a tax year, or three months or more on average over the period of absence, subject to a maximum of four years.

This status will apply from the day following your departure until the day preceding the day you return. This rule also applies to your spouse if he or she goes abroad with you. Therefore, provided one spouse works overseas and satisfies the above requirements, the accompanying spouse will also be regarded as non-resident and not ordinarily resident from the date of departure.

This means any UK income will be liable to UK income tax, whereas the overseas income will be completely exempt. From a capital gains tax perspective although you're non-UK resident and non-UK ordinarily resident, most overseas employees won't be able to escape UK CGT, as the scope of the CGT rules has been widened. There will be no UK capital gains tax on either UK or overseas assets owned at the date of departure, provided you are non-resident during the tax year of disposal and you remain overseas for a period of five complete tax years.

Note that this five-year rule does not apply to assets purchased after you become non-UK resident – you would be exempt from

UK capital gains tax on these provided you were non-resident during the tax year of disposal.

Example

John is a UK resident and domiciled individual who works for a UK company. He has been offered a 12-month overseas secondment to work full time for the company's Ruritanian subsidiary company. The secondment is to commence on 1 November 2006 and John will return to the UK on 30 October 2007. Any problems?

The key problem here is that while John may satisfy the other requirements relating to working overseas, his absence from the UK does not span a complete tax year. This would therefore result in John being UK resident for the entire tax year and his overseas income being subject to UK income tax.

8.2   TAX-DEDUCTIBLE EXPENSES

Where an employee is resident and ordinarily resident in the UK and performs all work duties abroad, the cost of travelling abroad to take up the employment and returning to the UK on its termination is allowable as a tax deduction.

If travel is only partly for the above purpose, relief is restricted to the relevant part.

Where the overseas duties necessitate the expense of board and lodging for the employee outside the UK and this expense is met by the employer, no tax liability will arise for the employee on the payments made.

Where you have two or more jobs, the duties of one or more of which are performed totally or partly overseas, you are entitled to tax relief for the cost of travelling between the jobs where either or both places are outside the UK.

Where an employee works overseas for a continuous period of 60 days or more, the payment by the employer for a visit by the employee's spouse/children (including a return ticket) will not be taxable.

8.3   TAX-FREE TERMINATION PAYMENTS

A termination payment made to an employee can be partially free of tax provided the employer had no contractual obligation to make the payment. Assuming this is satisfied, Section 401 ITEPA 2003 will usually apply, and the first £30,000 of the termination payment will be tax free.

However where an employee has substantial foreign service it is possible to obtain additional relief and in certain circumstances to totally eliminate any UK income tax charge.

In order to totally shelter the payment from UK tax, the period of employment must include foreign service which includes:

- Three-quarters of the whole period of service.

- Where service has exceeded 10 years, the whole of the last 10 years.

- If more than 20 years' service, half the period plus 10 of the last 20 years.

Where these conditions are not met, the amount exempt after any other deductions (such as the £30,000 exemption) will be in the proportion of foreign service to total service. In other words, a straightforward pro rata of time spent overseas to UK employment.

Example

Johnny commences employment with XYZ Plc in January 1997. He spends two years working at the overseas office in Germany. He is made redundant in January 2006 and is to be offered £100,000 as an ex gratia termination payment.

As Johnny's foreign service does not meet the above criteria, the amount that will be exempt will be two-ninths.

Therefore the taxable amount will be calculated as follows:

Termination payment	*£100,000*
Less S401 exemption	*(£30,000)*
	£70,000
Less foreign service relief	
2/9 x £70,000	*(£15,556)*
Taxable receipt	*£54,444*

8.4 PROTECTING YOUR PROPERTY INVESTMENTS FROM THE TAXMAN

An individual who works abroad for a number of years may decide to keep a UK residence.

If the property is subsequently sold, will the gain be subject to UK capital gains tax?

Obviously if the individual satisfies the non-residence/ordinary residence criteria at the date of disposal then any gain will be outside the scope of UK capital gains tax.

If the individual is UK resident/ordinarily resident at the date of disposal, it is necessary to look at the application of the Principal Private Residence (PPR) relief, in anticipation of returning to the UK to live in the property.

The PPR relief provides full or partial relief from capital gains tax for an individual who has occupied a property as his main residence at some point during the period of ownership.

A gain on a property will be completely exempt from capital gains tax if an individual has occupied the property as his main residence throughout his entire period of ownership.

Where an individual has occupied a property as a residence for only part of his period of ownership, a proportion of the capital gain resulting on the disposal of the property is tax free.

This is calculated on the following basis:

Capital Gain x Occupation Period/Ownership Period

In addition to the period that an individual actually occupies a property as his residence, when calculating the period of occupation, there are certain deemed periods of occupation that are allowed to be taken into account.

Most notably, the last 36 months of ownership would always be deemed to be private occupation, irrespective of whether you actually occupied the property during this period. Please note that this relief will only apply where the property has been your main residence at some point during your ownership.

Therefore an individual does not need to reside in a property during the last 36 months of ownership in order to gain full exemption from capital gains tax on a subsequent disposal.

Example

Samantha purchased a property in December 1998 for £50,000. She lived in the property as her main residence until June 2004 when she decided to move in with her boyfriend.

The property was then left empty until June 2006 when she decided to dispose of it. Any gain on the property when disposed of in June 2006 would be fully exempt from capital gains tax.

She actually resided in the house until June 2004, and the period from June 2004 until June 2006 is covered by the last 36 months 'deemed occupation' rule.

A problem occurs if the 36 months rule does not fully cover the period when the property was not occupied (in other words, the taxable portion). What is the position then?

Fortunately, there is a special provision that relates to individuals working overseas.

Any period during which the owner works full time in an employment wholly outside the UK, provided that both before AND after those periods it was the owner's only or main residence, and assuming he had no other main residence, is deemed private occupation.

Example

Peter purchased a house in 1997 and lived in this as his main residence until 2003. He then travelled abroad until 2006.

On his return he should ensure that he resumes occupation of the property. His period spent overseas would then not restrict the availability of the PPR exemption when he sells the property.

Chapter 9

Making Use of Double Tax Relief

9.1 INTRODUCTION

UK residents have to pay UK tax on income from UK and overseas sources. To prevent overseas income being taxed twice – once abroad and again in the UK – relief is given in one of two ways:

- By deducting the overseas tax from the UK tax – this is known as credit relief or

- By charging to UK tax the net amount of overseas income received. In other words, the amount of foreign income after foreign tax has been deducted – this is known as expense relief.

9.2 CREDIT RELIEF

The overseas income is deemed to be the top slice of income for these purposes – in other words, potentially taxed at the higher rate of 40%. If there is more than one source of foreign income, double tax relief on each source must be considered separately.

The income with the highest overseas tax is treated as the top slice of overseas income.

Credit relief is given as the lower of:

- The UK tax on the overseas income
- The overseas tax

Remember that, as complex as the rules are, the principal objective is to ensure that you do not obtain as a tax credit more than the UK rate of tax.

Therefore, if the overseas tax was charged at 50%, with UK tax being 40%, you would obtain DTR at 40%. Similarly, if the overseas tax was charged at 20%, and UK tax is 40%, you would only obtain DTR at 20%. This is best illustrated by means of an example.

Example

Doug, a UK resident individual has the following income in the 2006/2007 tax year:

Salary from UK employment	*£39,420*
UK dividends	*£1,875*
Overseas bank interest	*£1,100 (50% foreign tax paid)*

His tax calculation would be:

Salary from UK employment	*£39,420*
Overseas income	*£1,100*
UK dividends	*£1,875*
Less personal allowance	*(£5,035)*
Taxable income	*£37,360*

The income tax levied on this taxable income would be reduced by double taxation relief (DTR).

As the overseas income will be subject to tax at the higher rate (because Doug's salary pushes him into the higher-rate tax band and the overseas income is regarded as the 'top slice' of income) we can calculate that the DTR will be the lower of

- *The UK tax on overseas income (40% x £1,100) = £440*
- *The overseas tax (50% x £1,100) = £550*

Therefore total DTR in this case would be £440, and this would be given as a credit against Doug's tax liability.

It should be noted that if Doug had a tax loss for the period (for example, if he were self employed and had established a trading loss for offset against his other income) then the credit relief described above would be of little use as there would be no tax liability to offset the DTR against. In such a situation, expense relief is most beneficial.

9.3   EXPENSE RELIEF

As stated above, expense relief operates in a totally different way to credit relief. Instead of a credit for overseas tax, the overseas tax is simply deducted from the income before it is subject to UK tax. In other words, it is a deduction from the income rather than the tax on the income.

In most circumstances, credit relief will be far more beneficial but where an individual has no tax charge against which credit relief can operate, expense relief will be better, as it will increase the amount of the loss.

The best way to illustrate this is by means of an example.

Example

Doug's tax position for the next tax year, 2007/2008, is as follows:

Overseas income (taxed at 50%)   *£1,500*
UK trading loss   *(£10,000)*

No DTR will be given and the trading loss of £8,500 (£10,000 - £1,500) can be carried forward against future profits of the business.

Expense relief provides a better outcome. It is calculated as the net amount of overseas income, in other words £1,500 less 50% overseas tax = £750.

This increases Doug's trading loss to £9,250 (in other words, £10,000 - £750).

9.4   UNDERLYING TAX

We've looked at the position of an *individual* receiving overseas income but it could easily be the case that a UK company is used to hold overseas investments. What difference would this make?

The above general rules would apply and the amount of DTR would usually be calculated in the same way. Companies are, however, subject to a number of special provisions, one of which is that when a UK company receives a dividend from overseas it is entitled to a more beneficial DTR regime than an individual.

Where an overseas company pays a dividend to a UK company, it will normally have suffered two types of overseas tax:

- Underlying tax, and

- Withholding tax

Relief for the foreign withholding tax is similar to that enjoyed by individuals. However, relief for underlying tax is only available to companies.

Underlying tax is simply the foreign corporation tax. Remember that dividends aren't tax deductible, so when a company pays a dividend, the profits that are used to pay that dividend will have already been taxed. The whole point of the underlying tax rules is to provide some relief for the overseas corporation tax that the company paying the dividend has suffered.

A UK company can only get relief for the underlying tax if it owns at least 10% of the overseas company. Basically, the amount of relief is based on the proportion of the profits that are paid out as a dividend.

The formula you would typically use would be:

$$\frac{Dividend\ (including\ any\ withholding\ tax)}{Profits} \quad x \quad Overseas\ Tax\ Paid$$

This will be much clearer after you've seen exactly how it operates in an example:

Example

A company called A Ltd receives a dividend of £90,000 (after a 10% withholding tax) from its wholly owned subsidiary B Ltd.

The accounts of B Ltd show profits after tax of £300,000 and a tax bill of £65,000.

The underlying tax relief is calculated as follows:

Actual dividend received	*£90,000*
Withholding tax	*£10,000*
Total	***£100,000***

Underlying tax:

£100,000/£300,000 x £65,000	*£21,667*

A Ltd will pay tax on a total dividend receipt of £121,667.

However, overseas tax of £31,667 (£21,667 + £10,000) has already been paid and will be deducted from any UK tax payable.

Underlying tax relief can be a complex area, particularly as there are numerous provisions that can restrict the offset in certain circumstances. There are also specific provisions to allow some relief for surplus underlying tax against other foreign dividends received by the company (or from other group companies).

Chapter 10

Tax Benefits of Offshore Trusts

10.1 INTRODUCTION

An offshore trust is a legal entity into which you can pass ownership and control of your assets. The assets are then managed by a trustee (such as a trusted firm of accountants or lawyers) in the interests of the beneficiaries (your family, for example). The person who puts the assets into the trust (the settlor) may have a variety of reasons for distancing himself or herself from the ownership of the assets. For example, to remain anonymous for personal or business purposes or to avoid tax.

Offshore trusts are usually set up in tax havens or low tax jurisdictions such as the Channel Islands.

Please note that you should only consider using offshore trusts (and other offshore structures) after receiving advice from a qualified professional who fully understands your personal circumstances.

10.2 HOW OFFSHORE TRUSTS ARE TAXED

A trust currently counts as non-resident for both income tax and capital gains tax purposes if all of the trustees are non-resident and the general administration of the trust is carried on abroad. However from April 6 2007, a trust would only be non-resident if either all the trustees were non-resident, or if some of the trustees are non-resident and the settlor was non-UK domiciled when the trust was set up.

As the trust is non-resident it is not usually subject to capital gains tax in respect of UK or overseas assets (in other words, the same as an individual). Subject to anti-avoidance legislation, offshore trusts are therefore capable of sheltering both UK and foreign capital gains.

As has been mentioned earlier in relation to individuals, non-residents are not subject to UK tax on foreign income and therefore, in the absence of anti-avoidance legislation, offshore trusts can shelter such income. However, trusts are subject to income tax if the source of the income is the UK (just as an individual would be). Different trusts pay tax at different rates, although the type of trust most likely to be used in offshore tax planning would be either a discretionary trust or an accumulation and maintenance trust.

These trusts would pay tax at an effective 25% on UK dividends and 40% on other income or gains.

10.3 CAPITAL GAINS TAX CONSEQUENCES

The disposal of assets into a trust is a chargeable disposal for capital gains tax purposes and therefore a capital gain would arise. As the settlor is deemed to be 'connected' with the trust, and proceeds would be deemed to be equivalent to the market value of the assets transferred, it would therefore not be possible to avoid capital gains tax by simply gifting the assets.

The most effective method of establishing a trust from a capital gains tax perspective would therefore be to invest cash and let the trustees use this to invest as they see fit (in accordance with the trust deed). As the asset gifted is cash it falls outside the scope of capital gains tax.

Another possibility would be to settle assets that have a low initial value but which are expected to show significant growth in value. For example, shares in a newly formed company. Any growth in the value of the shares would occur offshore and, subject to the anti-avoidance rules, be outside the scope of UK capital gains tax.

Example

Eric is considering purchasing a share in a small South African mining company for £100,000. He is hoping that the mine will strike gold and the shares will rocket in value. Rather than purchase the shares in his own name, he goes to see his solicitor and forms an offshore trust into which he settles the £100,000. The trust then purchases the shares in the South African company. Any increase in value of the company would be effectively tax free as the trust would be outside the scope of UK capital gains tax. However, as we shall see, matters are not always that simple.

10.4   INHERITANCE TAX CONSEQUENCES

A trust is subject to UK inheritance tax if the settlor was domiciled or deemed to be domiciled in the UK when he set up the trust.

Example

Stefano is of Italian domicile and has moved to Britain to expand his business into the UK. He has substantial assets in Italy and wishes to protect these from inheritance tax. If Stefano sets up an offshore trust, provided he is not UK domiciled at the date of creation, the overseas assets will be outside the scope of UK inheritance tax, irrespective of the fact that Stefano may later acquire a UK domicile.

The problem with an offshore discretionary trust is that it can lead to a large inheritance tax cost for a UK domiciled individual (non-UK domiciliaries are considered in detail below).

A transfer of assets to a discretionary trust is called a chargeable lifetime transfer (CLT). This means that a proportion of inheritance tax is paid during the settlor's lifetime.

There are a number of complex rules governing this area. However, in essence the available nil rate band remaining is deducted from the value of the gift (in other words, the assets transferred into the trust) and tax is payable at 20% or 25% depending on whether the trust or the settlor is to pay the tax.

There is also a regime for taxing the assets of the trust. This is necessary, as when you transfer assets into a discretionary trust they are taken out of your estate and are therefore not subject to inheritance tax along with other assets you own.

The 2006 Budget also extended the discretionary trust provisions to most lifetime transfers to other types of trusts (for example accumulation and maintenance trusts established for the education of grandchildren). However, most offshore trusts established would, in any case, usually be discretionary.

The inheritance tax consequences of this discretionary trust treatment are not straightforward and the calculation is pretty complex. What happens is that an effective rate of IHT is calculated based on the initial value of the trust (taking into account previous transfers and all reliefs) based on IHT payable at 6%.

Then when assets are distributed out of the trust, and on every tenth anniversary of the date the trust is set up, inheritance tax is payable on the amount distributed or the trust assets. This ensures that the trust is subject to a form of inheritance tax.

In summary, there are two main circumstances where a discretionary trust is free of inheritance tax:

- Where the trust is within the settlor's nil rate band and remains within the nil rate band for the following 10 anniversaries. The key problem with this trust is that its value is limited to the amount of the nil rate band (£285,000 for the 2006/2007 tax year).

  One possible planning use could be to use the trust as a holding device in which the value of funds initially settled is low and then perhaps distribute the funds before the trust's 10th anniversary. The benefit of this is that for an exit before the first 10-year anniversary, the rate of inheritance tax is based on the value of funds when the trust was created. In this case there would be no inheritance tax exit charge.

- Where the assets transferred into the trust are covered by an inheritance tax exemption such as Business Property Relief (BPR). This relief provides for a full or partial exemption from inheritance tax where 'business assets' are gifted. Typical business assets include assets used in a trade, shares in unquoted trading companies and certain commercial property. There are a number of other conditions that would need to be satisfied to successfully claim Business Property Relief.

10.5   DANGERS FOR UK DOMICILIARIES

There are two principal obstacles that UK domiciliaries have to overcome to shelter their income and gains through an offshore trust:

- Tax anti-avoidance legislation which attributes *income* to the settlor. The income of an offshore trust is assessable as the settlor's if the actual or potential beneficiaries include him, his spouse or minor children or if any of them receives a benefit.

- Anti-avoidance legislation which attributes *gains* to the settlor. The provisions attribute gains to the settlor where any 'defined persons' are actual or potential beneficiaries who receive a benefit from the trust. The term 'defined person' includes the settlor and his spouse, their children, their children's spouses, their grandchildren and their grandchildren's spouses. Clearly this is a particularly wide anti-avoidance provision (and is much wider than the definition for UK trusts, which only applies to the settlor, his spouse and his minor children).

10.6   WHEN AN OFFSHORE TRUST CAN SAVE YOU TAX

There are three main situations where it is still possible for an offshore trust to operate as a tax shelter for a UK domiciled settlor:

1. Where the Settlor is Dead

Clearly the rules attributing income and gains to the settlor cannot apply if he is dead. This could arise if a trust is formed under the terms of a will.

In this case the assets would secure a tax-free uplift in their base cost for capital gains tax purposes (as the assets would pass into the trust at the market value at the date of death). Of course the assets passing into the trust would be subject to any inheritance tax on death unless the value transferred falls within the nil rate band, or the assets are covered by any other inheritance tax reliefs (such as Business Property Relief).

Example

John's estate consisted of:

House	*£223,000*
Cash	*£62,000*
Shares	*£500,000*

On the assumption that the shares were in an unquoted trading company, they would qualify for Business Property Relief (BPR) and the inheritance tax position would be as follows:

House	*£223,000*
Cash	*£62,000*
Nil rate band	*-£285,000*
Shares	*£500,000*
BPR	*-£500,000*

Therefore the inheritance tax charge would be nil.

Any subsequent gain arising on a disposal by John's heirs would be subject to UK capital gains tax (assuming the heirs are UK resident).

By contrast, John could have inserted a provision in his will for the shares to be settled in a non-resident discretionary trust. Inheritance tax would not be an issue, as the shares would qualify for BPR and, although John was a UK domiciliary, the anti-avoidance provisions should not apply as he is dead.

Assuming a subsequent disposal of the shares at a significant gain this would be outside the scope of UK capital gains tax as the gain would now be realised by a non-resident trust.

2. Trusts With All Defined Persons Excluded

Trusts where 'defined persons' are all excluded would not be subject to the anti-avoidance provisions attributing income or gains of the trust to the settlor. However, this is difficult to achieve because, for capital gains tax purposes, defined persons include the settlor, his spouse, children, grandchildren and all their spouses. Therefore, in order to totally exclude all defined persons, the trust would only be able to benefit your friends or remote relations (nephews, nieces etc).

A particular use may be where assets are expected to increase in value rapidly. The initial funds required may be low and an individual could persuade a friend to contribute the initial funds.

Due to the low initial value of the assets, there is unlikely to be any inheritance tax payable on the transfer, and any chargeable gain to date could be deferred in terms of Section 260 of the Income and Corporation Taxes Act, provided the settlor was not a beneficiary.

In this case, the settlor would be your friend and you would be the beneficiary.

The anti-avoidance provisions should not apply provided the settlor (in other words, the friend) does not benefit from the trust and he funds the initial cash required out of his own pocket and not under any agreement, for example in order to receive a future benefit.

The trust would therefore be capable of achieving the capital gains tax and income tax advantages mentioned above including an exemption from CGT on a subsequent disposal, without the gain being apportioned back to the UK resident settlor.

3. Grandchildren's Settlements

You could establish an offshore trust for the benefit of grandchildren and this would still be an effective shelter of foreign income, although not foreign gains. (This arises as the anti-avoidance provisions applying to capital gains tax are much wider than the income tax provisions.) Common assets for the trust to hold would be either shares in a non-resident trading company or a portfolio invested abroad for income.

Example

Peter, a UK resident and domiciled individual, settles cash in an offshore trust for the benefit of his grandchildren who are UK resident. He and his wife are specifically excluded from the class of beneficiaries in the trust deed. The trustees use the cash to purchase shares in a UK company. Any dividends received by the offshore trust would not be liable to UK income tax. Clearly if a UK trust was used, UK income tax would be fully chargeable on dividends received.

This would then allow a tax-free roll up of funds offshore. If the trust were to pay a distribution to the UK-resident grandchildren, UK tax would be payable, although the grandchildren would always have the option of becoming non-resident themselves and obtaining the cash free of UK tax during a year of non-residency (for example, by taking a 'year out').

If the trustees were to sell some of the shares, the gains would be apportioned to Peter as he was the settlor and because the beneficiaries include individuals from an excluded class.

10.7   UK RESIDENT BUT NOT UK DOMICILED

In the absence of a trust, the best strategy for a non-domiciliary is to keep his investments (along with any income/proceeds) outside the UK. In this way any income tax/capital gains tax liability is avoided under the remittance basis, and inheritance tax only applies to his UK assets/estate.

There are, however, a number of problems with this approach, in particular the deemed domicile rules may apply for inheritance tax purposes and treat the individual as UK domiciled for inheritance tax purposes. This would have the effect of subjecting his worldwide estate to UK inheritance tax. There is also, of course, the risk that the individual creates sufficient intention to stay in the UK that he obtains a UK domicile.

Use of a trust could help to avoid these risks. If a non-UK domiciliary establishes a trust of which he is a beneficiary, the property in the trust is termed 'excluded property' provided:

• The settlor was not UK domiciled (or deemed domiciled) at the time the trust was established, and

• The trust property is situated outside of the UK.

Example

Terry, a UK resident, but of US domicile, has been resident in the UK for 15 years. He owns substantial assets in both the UK and the US and eventually intends to move back to the US and enjoy his retirement. Once Terry has been resident in the UK for 17 years he will have deemed domicile. This will mean that in the event of his untimely death, the whole of his estate would be taxed in accordance with the UK inheritance tax legislation. If Terry was to transfer his non-UK assets into a trust now (in other words, before he is deemed UK domiciled), the American assets would be excluded property and outside the scope of UK inheritance tax .

Capital Gains Tax

An excluded property settlement also has a number of advantages from a capital gains tax perspective.

Under the current rules, provided the trustees aren't UK resident and the administration of the trust is carried on overseas, the trust is not subject to UK capital gains tax (unless the UK assets of the trust are used in a UK branch/agency trade).

Tax anti-avoidance rules will attribute the gains of the trust to any UK settlor/beneficiary and the trust gains are treated as their individual gains.

However, when the settlor/beneficiary is non-resident or non-UK domiciled these rules do not apply and therefore, provided the settlor remains non-domiciled, any trust gains are outside the UK capital gains tax net.

Therefore the use of an overseas trust is expanded for non-UK domiciliaries as the anti-avoidance provisions are limited in scope.

The remittance of proceeds would be a capital distribution from the trust to a UK resident individual. The tax treatment of this would depend on how it was structured, and professional advice is essential. A straightforward remittance by a UK resident would be likely to be within the scope of UK tax. One option would be to retain the funds offshore and make a gift to a spouse or other relative. They could then bring the funds into the UK, free of UK capital gains tax and potentially free of UK income tax.

Example

Joe a UK resident, but with Greek domicile, settles some assets into an offshore discretionary trust. If the trust later sells the assets at a gain of £1 million there will be no UK capital gains tax charge. The anti-avoidance provisions will not attribute the gain to Joe (as he is non-UK domiciled) and provided any beneficiaries of the trust are also non-UK domiciled, none of the gain will be attributed to them either.

This will apply to both UK and overseas assets settled into the trust.

Income Tax

Again the anti-avoidance provisions are amended, the effect of which can be that any UK income of the trust is taxed as the settlor's, whereas foreign income could be subject to the remittance basis and may escape UK income tax, provided the income is kept overseas by the trustees. If the settlor beneficiary subsequently acquires a UK domicile:

- The inheritance tax position of the trust remains the same (in other words, provided the property is situated overseas, then the trust property is outside the scope of UK inheritance tax).

- For capital gains tax, any gains of the trust would become taxed on the settlor as they arise.

- The worldwide income of the trust would be taxed on the settlor.

Example

Eduardo, who was originally born in Latvia, has been UK resident for the last 15 years. He made good use of the benefits of being a non-UK domiciliary as regards offshore trusts and has established such trusts, which now contain significant assets.

He is in the process of disposing of the last of his Latvian assets and is concerned that, given his particular circumstances, he may be classed as having UK domicile.

This would be disastrous for Eduardo and income and gains of the trust would be taxable.

In such circumstances, forward thinking is always beneficial.

In the tax year before the change in domicile the trust could distribute sufficient cash to support Eduardo's lifestyle. They would then be excluded from the trust and the anti-avoidance provisions would not attribute income (and gains provided other relevant beneficiaries are excluded) to Eduardo.

Sheltering from Overseas Tax

Depending on the overseas country's domestic tax rules, using an overseas trust can help to minimise overseas tax, particularly inheritance tax, and prevent the establishment of an overseas estate.

Example

David, a non-UK domiciliary is considering investing in property in South Africa. If he uses the offshore trust/company structure, the big advantage is that he will not be regarded as owning South African assets. As such he will not be subject to overseas inheritance tax, and will not be subject to the South African estate laws.

10.8   WHERE DO YOU SET UP A TRUST AND HOW MUCH DOES IT COST?

There are numerous countries that offer an attractive regime for setting up an offshore trust. A trust may be set up or administered anywhere in the world. However, it's essential that the jurisdiction in which the trust is established recognises the legal concept of the trust. The countries listed below all recognise the use of trusts.

The four main reasons for setting up a trust are to:

- Protect your assets from creditors etc
- Maintain confidentiality
- Avoid financial reporting requirements
- Pay less tax

The countries listed below are all recognised as good places to locate an offshore trust. This list is by no means exhaustive and, depending on how the trust will be used and the location of the beneficiaries and the settlor, other countries such as Mauritius and Belize could also be considered.

When choosing where to set up your trust, other significant non-tax considerations could be paramount including the:

- Language used in the jurisdiction.
- Time difference between you and the trust jurisdiction.
- Political and financial stability of the country.
- Geographic proximity – in case you need to travel there.
- Fees associated with setting up and maintaining the trust.

For example an individual looking at significant trade with China could envisage a trust in Mauritius as opposed to St Kitts, due to the former's close relationship with China.

However, the top locations where a trust can be established at an affordable price are as follows:

- Jersey
- Liechtenstein
- The Cayman Islands
- St Kitts Nevis
- Panama
- Gibraltar
- Isle of Man
- Bermuda
- Bahamas
- Austria
- New Zealand

Obviously financial costs are incurred in setting up and running an offshore trust. It is likely to cost from £1,000-plus for the initial set up and further charges will be incurred for ongoing compliance work and if you require professional advisers to act as trustees.

Please note that, while there are many reputable firms offering offshore tax planning services, there are also many fly-by-night operators providing advice of dubious

quality that may land you in considerable trouble with the UK taxman.

It should also be noted that the settlor and beneficiaries of an offshore trust must disclose all relevant information on their tax returns. In addition, when the trust is established the person making the settlement MUST submit a return to Revenue and Customs within three months.

10.9   USING TRUSTS FOR ASSET PROTECTION

Offshore trusts are popular, not just as tax-saving devices, but also for their perceived *asset protection* benefits.

Many wealthy individuals fear being sued and losing a significant chunk of their wealth. If your assets are visible or easily reached, you are pretty much a sitting duck these days.

Because of this danger many wealthy individuals set up offshore structures to hide their assets or make them difficult to plunder.

A wide variety of people engage in asset protection planning but it's particularly popular with those working in professions where there is a higher risk of litigation:

- Doctors
- Lawyers
- Accountants
- Builders
- Consultants
- Financial advisers

Asset protection planning is also popular with those who want to safeguard their money from ex-spouses and other family members, disgruntled employees and business partners.

The bottom line is this: those with deep pockets are perceived as easy prey nowadays. Asset-protection planning acts like a castle moat, protecting your hard-earned wealth from the outside world.

Asset protection measures can be split into three main categories:

Insurance

Pretty obvious in itself, but having good insurance can save a lot of worry. In fact, most professionals or traders are required to have indemnity insurance to cover them against providing negligent advice or faulty goods and services. Although insurance provides a good 'base' level of protection it's unlikely that any policy will cover the full range of potential claims and other more comprehensive asset protection tools are often needed.

Limiting Your Liability

Another way to protect your assets is to set up a company. A company has a separate legal identity, which means in principle any creditors would have to target the company's assets, rather than your own. And if the company doesn't have any assets then the claim will amount to nothing.

However, the courts can and do 'pierce the corporate veil' in certain circumstances. This means they will ignore the limited liability protection provided by the company and instead seek to recover the personal assets of the shareholders or directors.

This is something you would have to discuss with your solicitor, however there are a number of situations where limited liability protection does not work. For example, the Insolvency Act contains special provisions which cover fraudulent trading or wrongful trading.

Essentially, if you carry on trading and incurring liabilities when you know or have reason to believe the company can't pay its debts, the creditors can target your personal assets.

Other situations where the veil can be pierced are:

- Where the use of a company is a sham and it is used for fraudulent purposes.

- Where a 'special relationship' existed between a director of the company and the customer so that the customer relied on a personal assumption of responsibility by the director.

Using a company may not provide any additional protection against such personal claims. However, it could be used to reduce the risk of general business claims.

There are several types of entity that can be used for limited liability protection, including a limited company and a limited liability partnership.

An alternative (especially when combined with the wealth segregation activities discussed below) is to consider using an offshore entity such as a limited liability company (LLC). An LLC has fewer requirements (compulsory annual meetings, directors etc). However, given it is overseas, it would cost much more to set up than a UK company (which can be set up for around £100). We look at the different types of entity in the next chapter.

Ring-fencing Your Assets

Another option is to look at separating your wealth from your estate. In effect, this means putting it outside the reach of any creditors.

The simplest way to protect an asset is by ensuring that you don't own it any more – by giving it away, for example. However, if this is a sham arrangement, and you still have control over the asset or have use of it (for example, if you occupy a property that you have given away) a court is likely to rule that you have retained the 'beneficial interest' and the asset will be classed as part of your estate.

Using a company is also a way of segregating assets, as by transferring to a company, you are also divesting yourself of ownership. As seen above, the courts can and do ignore the company in certain circumstances. This is why many individuals looking to exclude some of their wealth from their estates use offshore arrangements in countries that have strict privacy laws.

If you set up an offshore company to hold your assets you should try and avoid becoming a shareholder in the company. If you are a shareholder a court is likely to class the value of the shares/company assets as part of your estate.

Note that this is different from simply keeping quiet about the existence of the company. If you choose correctly you can ensure that shareholder details aren't named on any share register, and if they are, it's only the legal owner that is named. You could then use nominees to hold the legal title to the shares, keeping your name off the documents.

Many people do this and are successful on the basis that any creditors would need to find the assets before they can have a slice of them. One point that is worth noting here is that if the segregated assets were to generate any income, this would need to be disclosed on your UK tax return if you are UK resident and domiciled (this would then make it practically impossible to deny the existence of the offshore assets).

That is why, in terms of asset protection, the use of a trust and company is more common than an offshore company on its own.

In a trust arrangement, the settlor gives control of his assets to trustees, who manage and control the trust assets for the beneficiaries (who can include the settlor). Although the settlor will usually provide a letter of wishes, indicating how he would like the trust to operate and the kind of distributions that should be made, it is the trustees that have legal control over the assets.

Trusts could traditionally be used to 'break the link' between an individual and his assets and, although this is now less the case, they can still be effective for this purpose.

The courts take a practical approach to the matter and if you set up a trust, make yourself one of the beneficiaries and receive significant distributions on a regular basis, don't be surprised if a court classes the assets as yours.

This isn't to say that it's not worthwhile using the trust as the offshore nature would undoubtedly make it more difficult to enforce. However, to be on the safe side, you would be better off if you weren't a beneficiary and received only a limited amount of income from the trust.

Similarly, ensuring that the trustees do not automatically agree to all your requests would also assist in preventing the assets being classed as yours. Basically you want to avoid any argument that the trustees are just 'rubber stamping' any request or direction you give them.

Using Offshore Trusts to Protect Assets on Divorce

Many high net worth individuals realise that nowadays a marriage breakdown could pose a massive threat to their wealth. As a result they use offshore structures to protect their assets.

By using a trust spouses facing divorce can simply argue that they are merely discretionary beneficiaries of the trust and that the trust assets should not be treated as their own.

The courts don't always accept this and have the power to go after trust assets when they are made in contemplation of marriage or during the marriage. The terms are widely interpreted and include both UK and offshore trusts.

Even if a trust is not regarded as being made in contemplation of marriage, a court will usually take into account the history of any receipts from the trusts.

Therefore if there has been a regular income stream, a court would usually take the view that the income would continue (even if it stops at the time of the divorce).

Courts also have wide powers to order disclosure of information relating to trusts as trustees can be asked to be joined as parties to legal proceedings. The main purpose of this would be to get information about the trust from the trustees. This is why *offshore* trusts are popular, as enforcing decisions against offshore trustees is usually more difficult.

Instead, if there are sufficient other assets available, the court may prefer to order a transfer of those assets given that it is much simpler and more cost effective than chasing after assets in an offshore trust. Even so, the value of the offshore trust could be taken into account.

Offshore trusts can be useful vehicles but it is all too easy to think that they can always protect assets on divorce. As shown above, even if your spouse is not a beneficiary a court may well be able to amend a trust to effectively grant them some of the trust assets.

If you are considering using an offshore trust you should, wherever possible, ensure that there is no expectation of a receipt from the trust. Also, be warned that if you're thinking of setting up a trust and transferring your assets into it in case you suffer a marriage breakdown, a court would not look favourably on the arrangement.

In terms of greater security, a person at risk of divorce should, wherever possible, not be a beneficiary of the trust – the spouse should also not be a beneficiary.

This will prevent the trust assets being treated as part of their assets. In addition, it would also make actually getting hold of trust documents more difficult (as only beneficiaries and trustees would usually have a right to see trust documents).

Similar considerations also apply to other asset protection strategies, for example protecting against potential creditors

Rather than use an offshore entity, many individuals use an offshore bank account to hold their cash. There is no real segregation of wealth here as the cash still plainly belongs to you. This is therefore purely a case of 'hiding' the cash and hoping no one finds out about it. Given that banking secrecy laws in offshore jurisdictions are usually very strict, unless criminal activity or money laundering is suspected, it's unlikely that your details will be made available to a third party.

You would need to ensure that any income generated from the offshore account is declared on your tax return. If you don't, you then need to consider the impact of the EU Savings Tax Directive in terms of which the UK tax authorities would be informed of the income, or tax will be withheld from any interest paid.

You should also note that Revenue and Customs is clamping down on people who aren't declaring interest earned from overseas bank accounts. It goes without saying that hiding income from the taxman is not a very clever offshore strategy and you should always disclose when you have to.

Asset protection for UK residents is a complex area and the best course of action is to take advice from a lawyer with experience in this area.

10.10 KEEPING A LOW PROFILE

An issue that is related to asset protection is the desire to keep your activities private and avoid intrusion into your affairs.

It's for this reason you need to be mindful as to how your actions are monitored by the authorities.

A good example relates to a colleague of mine. He is a non-UK resident (living in Gibraltar) and has most of his cash and investments outside the UK. However, as he buys a lot of goods from auction websites in the UK, he established a UK bank account to obtain a UK debit card.

However, he was finding purchases of airline tickets and other goods increasingly difficult using a non-UK shipping address. He decided, therefore, to use a UK friend's house as the registered and shipping address.

After he transferred a couple of thousand pounds into the account from overseas he received a letter from the HMRC Compliance Division. The authorities were concerned about the unmatched nature of the account. All information is cross checked these days and when you have cash coming in from overseas to a UK individual, the authorities make sure it ties in with their records.

Of course there was nothing sinister about my colleague's arrangement but the worrying aspect for most people is having to explain to Big Brother how you choose to structure your financial affairs.

There are a number of transactions that can 'red flag' you to the authorities. Some of the more common activities are:

Anything Unusual

In short, anything unusual can set the alarm bells ringing, such as large or frequent transactions from overseas. The UK authorities are pretty paranoid about the 'offshore angle' at the moment, so any unusually large or frequent transfers from overseas will be initially viewed with an element of suspicion.

We're not even talking about massive sums of money. Banks are required to report irregular account activity, so if you normally tick along with an account balance of £1,000 and suddenly £10,000 is transferred into your account from overseas, you may find that you need to explain where the funds came from.

As well as the size of transactions there is also the number of transactions. If you normally use your account for just receiving salary and paying a few direct debits but then suddenly start having lots of Paypal transfers from your Ebay dealings, don't be surprised if you later receive a letter from the UK taxman if you have not been declaring any trading income.

Unmatched Information

As above, if you set yourself up a network of offshore companies, offshore bank accounts and trusts, you need to be careful that the declared signatories, including trustees and directors, all have verifiable addresses. As seen above, if you use an address that is not registered to you, or rather is registered to someone else, the authorities may pick up on this, particularly if there are also transfers of funds from overseas.

Transferring Assets Overseas

The UK taxman doesn't like assets going outside the UK tax net, so one area the Government agencies keep a close eye on is overseas asset transfers. Pretty obvious really but if you're looking to fund an offshore company, simply transferring the cash from your UK bank account may not be advisable if you're wanting to keep your affairs private. This kind of paper trail will undoubtedly result in the UK authorities knowing about your offshore account.

Offshore Companies

Using an offshore company is a perfectly legitimate commercial and tax-planning strategy. However, as with most strategies, you need to use these with your eyes wide open.

What most of the various offshore incorporation agents (people that set up offshore companies) fail to tell you is that if you use a company established in certain tax havens, this in itself could make the UK authorities take a closer look at your affairs.

Actually deciding which jurisdictions could red flag your activities is difficult, although countries such as Colombia, Ecuador, Russia, Latvia, Thailand, Nigeria, the Cayman Islands, Liechtenstein and Pakistan could be considered higher risk than other jurisdictions.

It's for this reason that the nominee structure has grown in popularity. Essentially, this involves using a company formed in a respected jurisdiction to be the commercial 'face' of the group's activities. The tax haven company would then be a holding company and funds would be channelled to the tax haven. The UK is one of the most popular destinations for nominee companies, given its sound economy, strong international links, low corporate taxation and good double tax treaty network.

The nominee structure works by ensuring that any invoicing comes from the nominee company. A UK customer, for example, may be happier receiving an invoice from a UK company than an overseas company. The UK company would receive the cash and then, as per the nominee agreement, the majority of the funds would be transferred to the overseas company.

It would be important for the UK nominee to retain some income to ensure that this overall structure is viewed as an above-board commercial agreement and usually the nominee would receive an agent's fee calculated on an arm's length basis.

Chapter 11

Tax Benefits of Offshore Companies

11.1 INTRODUCTION

A UK resident company is subject to UK corporation tax on its worldwide income and gains. By contrast a non-UK resident company is only subject to corporation tax on its UK income.

At first glance, therefore, it would seem that an offshore company is an effective way of sheltering income and capital gains from the taxman, as all foreign income and gains accruing to the company should be free of UK tax.

In fact using a *directly owned* offshore company is not a straightforward option to avoid UK taxes. One of the reasons for this is the issue of 'deemed' company residence. A company is regarded as a UK resident if:

- It is a UK incorporated company, or
- Its *central management and control* is in the UK.

Various legal cases have indicated that it is the function of the board of directors to run the company and therefore Revenue and Customs would initially be concerned with where the board of directors meet, when they meet, and whether they actually exercise control over the company and make management decisions.

So if a board of directors meet overseas and review management decisions and strategies this should constitute overseas central management and control.

However, where there is a controlling shareholder in the UK there is a risk that the directors will not correctly exercise their authority over the company with the result that HMRC may argue that the company is run by the controlling shareholder in the UK. In these circumstances the company would be classed as UK resident and subject to UK corporation tax.

11.2 HOW THE TAXMAN SPOTS
PHONY OFFSHORE MANAGEMENT

HMRC has stated that it will look at offshore companies to identify if there has been an attempt to create simply the appearance of central management and control in a place.

Therefore, care is needed to ensure that any overseas directors are actually running the company.

In order to pass the central management and control test the majority of the directors should be non-UK resident, and the non-UK resident directors should actively participate in making board decisions.

This therefore means that key business decisions should be taken at overseas board meetings. A UK resident shareholder may therefore establish a non-resident company but it is essential to ensure that the running of the business is left to the non-resident directors.

The central management and control test was looked at by the High court and the Court of Appeal in the 2005 case *Wood v Holden*. The taxpayer in this case successfully argued that the central management and control of an offshore company was overseas.

The facts were complex but essentially a Dutch subsidiary was incorporated which was part of a tax planning scheme. It acquired some shares in a UK company and HMRC felt that, as there was no real business being carried on overseas, the Dutch company should be taxed as a UK resident company.

The appeal commissioners sided with HMRC and took the view that " ... the company resides for purposes of income tax where its real business is carried on where the central control and management actually abides...".

However, both the High Court and the Court of Appeal decided this was wrong. They said that the directors who were non-resident were not sidestepped or bypassed and there was no evidence that UK parties dictated to them. The overseas directors actually executed the board meetings and resolutions. Therefore, in the absence of any evidence showing them deferring to other parties, they and the company were non-resident.

This case reinforced the fact that it is essential that overseas directors actually consider the board resolutions and other transactions in order to evidence the fact that they are not under the control of another person. Note that an overseas shareholder having influence over the directors is fine, but there is a problem when the directors simply accept everything the shareholder says and carry out his wishes without any consideration.

11.3   APPORTIONMENT OF CAPITAL GAINS

UK tax anti-avoidance provisions require the gains of a non-resident 'close' company to be apportioned amongst the member shareholders. Capital gains tax is charged on those who are resident and, in the case of individuals, domiciled in the UK.

The definition of a close company can be complex, however in simple terms it applies to a company that is controlled by its directors or five or fewer shareholders.

Example

Jack and Jill are the sole shareholders of JackJill Ltd, a company registered in the Cayman Islands. They hold 50% of the shares each and are both UK resident and domiciled. Assuming they allow non-resident directors to run the company and can satisfactorily show that the company is not centrally managed and controlled from the UK, then the attribution of gains legislation would mean that any gains of the offshore company would be attributed to Jack and Jill (50% each). However, if Jack was non-UK domiciled, the gains would NOT be attributed to him, only to Jill.

11.4   BENEFITS IN KIND

If Revenue and Customs is able to assert that the company is being managed by the shareholder or that the directors of the company are accustomed to act on his directions, he will be classed as a shadow director and income tax will be payable on any benefit in kind received by him or his family. One of the key benefits in kind that may apply is the accommodation charge. This levies a charge on an employee where he or she is provided with accommodation by an employer.

11.5   USING A NON-RESIDENT TRUST AND COMPANY

For the reasons stated above, offshore companies that are directly owned by UK residents are not actually that common in practice. Instead, offshore companies *owned by offshore trusts* are used more frequently. Such arrangements are often popular from a non-tax angle due to the practical advantages of owning the trust investments through one or more wholly owned offshore companies. This gives the trustees the benefit of limited liability.

The residence of the company is not a key issue in these circumstances as the only persons legally entitled to exercise control of the company are the non-resident trustees. However, following on from the *Wood v Holden* case, care would need to be taken to ensure that the company really is run by either the trustees or directors. If they were to stand aside and let a settlor/beneficiary give all the instructions, it could be contended that the company residence is the same as that of the settlor or beneficiary.

Provided the beneficiaries were non-resident, they would suffer no UK taxation charge on distributions from the trust, and the company/trust would also suffer no UK tax charge if the assets held were overseas assets. If the beneficiary is a UK resident, the main problem would be the UK anti-avoidance legislation. There would be no real way of escaping this, although if one of the exemptions applied (for example, the motive test) satisfied, this could be claimed on the tax return.

The motive test is an important aspect of one of the key anti-avoidance rules that attributes the income of offshore trusts and companies to UK resident individuals. The anti-avoidance provisions will not apply if the transfer overseas was not made for the purpose of avoiding tax or if there was a real commercial reason for transferring assets to an overseas company or trust.

Therefore for an individual to take advantage of this rule, and claim that income from an offshore company or trust should not be attributed to them, they would need to show that there was no tax avoidance motive in the transfer of any asset overseas and essentially that the companies were located overseas for sound commercial reasons. This can be a difficult provision to satisfy.

In order to be non-resident for income tax and capital gains tax purposes under the current rules the trustees would all need to be non-resident and the general administration of the trust would need to be carried on abroad.

Example

Peter, a UK resident and domiciled individual wishes to purchase a business and property in Ibiza. One option would be to establish a trust, and transfer funds to the trustees. They would then either purchase the property directly, or via a wholly owned company.

The transfer of funds from Peter would, however, be a problem from an inheritance tax perspective. As Peter is UK domiciled, the settlement is an immediately chargeable transfer, taxable at 20% for amounts above £285,000 (this assumes that he has made no previous gifts). However, the advantage of using a discretionary trust route is that the property would then be excluded from his estate for inheritance tax purposes. The drawback is that the trust would be subject to a separate regime of UK taxation. For inheritance tax purposes, the trust is subject to UK inheritance tax if Peter was domiciled in the UK when the transfer was made. This would undoubtedly be the case.

In these circumstances one option to exempt the trust from UK inheritance tax would be for the transfer to the trust to be of 'relevant business property'. The transfer to the trust would then be exempt from UK inheritance tax, and the trust itself would not suffer an ongoing inheritance tax charge, as business property relief (BPR) would exclude the property from the inheritance tax charge.

Relevant business property includes a sole trader business, assets used in a partnership and shares in unquoted trading companies. Therefore in this case it would be far better for Peter to purchase the business and property directly and subsequently transfer this to the trust/company.

Provided any transfer was made shortly afterwards, there would be unlikely to be a capital gains tax charge as any increase in value would be minimal.

The trust would then be exempt from UK inheritance tax as the assets transferred would qualify for Business Property Relief.

11.6   USING AN OFFSHORE COMPANY & TRUST: NON-UK DOMICILIARIES

Many non-UK domiciliaries choose to use this structure to minimise their UK tax liabilities.

Example

Paul is a non-UK domiciliary and wishes to purchase a property in the Isle of Man (IOM). He decides to use an offshore company to own the property with 100% of the shares in the company owned by a non-resident IOM trust. The tax implications are as follows:

Capital Gains Tax

As non-residents the trust and company will not be subject to UK capital gains tax. Provided the beneficiaries are non-UK domiciled, any distribution to the beneficiary could be taxed on the remittance basis.

Income Tax

Any foreign income earned by the trust is not subject to UK income tax, unless it is remitted to the UK. If the trust/company was to own UK property, the income would, however, be taxable. The anti-avoidance provisions will apply if Paul or his spouse or children can benefit from the trust. In this case, he may be taxed on the UK income as it arises (whether remitted or not).

Inheritance Tax

The Isle of Man trust is only subject to UK inheritance tax on UK assets, as it was established by a non-UK domiciled individual. By using the offshore company to hold any UK property, there will be no UK inheritance tax on the property, as the trust will hold shares in an IOM company, which are treated as non-UK assets for inheritance tax purposes.

Non-UK Domiciled Spouse

Where one spouse is a UK domiciliary, and the other is not, it is still possible for the UK domiciliary's assets to be protected by transferring assets to a non-UK domiciliary. However, whereas a normal inter-spouse transfer between UK domiciliaries is exempt from UK inheritance tax, a transfer from a UK domiciliary to his non-UK domiciled spouse is only exempt on the first £55,000 of value transferred. If the £55,000 limit is exceeded, this would be treated as a 'potentially exempt transfer' and exempt from inheritance tax provided the spouse making the gift survives seven years from the date of the transfer.

The non-domiciled spouse could then establish the offshore trust and company structure. The benefits outlined above would then arise. Note that the inter-spouse transfer must not be made subject to any form of condition or immediately prior to the establishment of the offshore structure.

11.7   PERSONAL SERVICE COMPANIES

With the advent of email and the internet many people trading through UK companies are wanting to move abroad.

One way for them to 'have their cake and eat it' is to use an offshore employment company.

Using this they would move overseas and become an employee of the offshore company. The offshore company would then charge the UK trading company for the services provided to the UK company.

The UK company should be able to claim this expense as a tax deduction and the offshore company would receive income on which no tax would be payable. Funds could then be extracted from the offshore company by way of a dividend.

100

Multinationals use this on a larger scale and use offshore employment companies as a vehicle to provide expatriate staff, who work outside both their home country and the offshore jurisdiction, with almost tax-free remuneration.

Example

Paddy runs his own business through a UK incorporated company (Paddy Limited). He is fed up with the British climate and taxes and decides to move overseas.

He settles in the Bahamas and establishes a company in Panama. He still provides services for Paddy Limited and invoices the company accordingly. Assuming he is the only employee, and the company has profits of £200,000 before paying him, he may decide that the market rate for his services is £150,000 and raise an invoice for this amount from the Panamanian company.

The UK company's taxable profits will be reduced to £50,000, and the £150,000 received by the Panamanian company will not be taxed.

An alternative scenario would be for Paddy to remain an employee of the UK company and perform his duties overseas.

As discussed previously, a non-UK resident individual performing employment duties offshore will not be subject to UK income tax. National insurance should also not be due provided the individual is not UK ordinarily resident. As above, the company should also be allowed a tax deduction for the salary paid.

Note that in both of these situations it is absolutely essential that a market rate is used. HMRC has some complex rules known as the transfer pricing rules that could otherwise apply.

11.8   TRANSFER PRICING RULES

These rules apply where a UK resident is dealing with a non-resident and are intended primarily to prevent companies from manipulating prices to reduce UK taxable profits.

Without these rules it would be easy for a multinational group to arrange for its overseas companies to charge increased amounts for parts, stock or services so as to reduce taxable profits in the UK.

Therefore when a UK resident is dealing with offshore entities, an 'arm's length' rate must be used. This means that if you move offshore and invoice a UK company or charge a salary, the rate you charge must be the same as what would be charged by an unconnected third party providing those services.

You would also need to retain evidence of the third party rate, in case HMRC ever enquires into the matter.

Under self assessment it is for the company to establish and support the fact that an arm's length basis is used. However, HMRC accepts that there may be circumstances where establishing the arm's length rate will be difficult. The transfer pricing provisions therefore provide for a procedure known as 'advance pricing agreements' (APAs).

An APA is a written agreement between a business and HMRC which determines a method for resolving transfer pricing issues in advance of a tax return being made.

It's important to adhere to the provisions of the APA as not only are there potential penalties at stake, but the tax authorities could also restrict the deduction the UK company can claim if it is felt that you have charged an excessive amount.

Advanced offshore arrangements should be carefully considered. They frequently involve a complex interaction of many taxation issues, and professional advice will need to be taken.

11.9   TYPES OF OFFSHORE ENTITY

When looking at the various options available to you to structure your affairs you'll find that there are a number of different entities – both onshore and offshore – that can be used. It can be difficult to understand the differences between the various options so we'll look briefly at each.

UK Limited Company (Ltd)

This is your bog standard company used by traders and investors. It can be used to hold pretty much all assets and can carry out most activities.

When you form the company you'll need to provide some details to both Companies House and later HMRC. Note that any UK incorporated company is automatically classed as UK resident and is therefore taxed in the UK on its worldwide income.

UK Ltd companies are very cheap to form and ongoing administration is not too onerous. You'll need to file annual accounts in a suitable format, and also submit the annual return (which contains details of the company and shareholders).

In terms of asset protection it can be a good way to hold assets separately although, as we've seen, the courts can ignore the company where the arrangement looks like a sham, so you'll need to ensure that there is commercial substance.

If you're looking to trade overseas, a UK company has the advantage of looking highly professional and would not draw attention to your activities, unlike companies registered in certain tax havens. Therefore using a UK Ltd nominee company is popular, to combine a professional front with minimising taxes.

The Ltd company is a separate entity from its shareholders. It can therefore sue or be sued in its own name and will be treated for tax purposes separately from its directors and shareholders. One of the main purposes of forming a Ltd company can be to minimise UK taxes.

UK companies pay UK corporation tax as opposed to UK income tax and for most this will mean paying corporation tax at 19% as opposed to 40% income tax. Provided only limited profits are then extracted from the company (for example, only enough to use up the basic-rate tax band) there would be no further tax to pay.

UK Limited Liability Partnership (LLP)

This is a cross between a Ltd company and a normal partnership. It was primarily introduced for the large professional firms that carried on a trade as a partnership (for example, lawyers, accountants and surveyors) but who wanted the benefit of limited liability protection.

Therefore an LLP allows the members to protect their personal assets from any creditors, but for tax purposes it is treated just like any other partnership. The LLP will be taxed on a 'pass through' basis with each partner being treated as owning a share in the partnership assets. The profits of the partnership would then be attributed to the partners, irrespective of whether the partners actually take their share of the profits out of the partnership or not.

For asset protection purposes it offers pretty much the same protection as a Ltd company. In tax terms the tax liability will depend on the partners' residence and other taxable income.

If an LLP is used with a mixture of UK and overseas partners, it would be only the UK partners that would be taxed in the UK, with the overseas partners being taxed in their country of residence. Where there are mixed residence partnerships an LLP may therefore be preferred to a UK company. Mixed residence partnerships also offer certain capital gains tax advantages (covered in the next chapter).

International Business Company (IBC)

This is the name typically given to an offshore company that has been formed outside the UK.

There are three main reasons that an IBC may be used.

- To avoid UK taxes

- To hide assets

- To trade overseas, either by UK or overseas residents.

Rather than using a simple offshore bank account, many people use an offshore account with the account holder being an IBC – the aim being to sever the link between the individual and the offshore assets.

As with UK companies, IBCs can be used for practically any purpose, including holding overseas property and shares, bank accounts and other assets.

Unlike UK companies, an IBC usually has much lower disclosure requirements with hardly any form filling, no annual accounts or returns and no annual general meeting. It's usually also exempt from local taxes provided you incorporate in a suitable jurisdiction.

Bearer Share Companies

There are a number of jurisdictions (such as the British Virgin Islands) that permit you to form a special bearer share company. This will cost you more than a standard company – but what benefit do you get for the extra cash?

A normal company lists the owner of the shares on the share certificates and when you want to transfer ownership of the shares you need to notify Companies House.

A bearer share company is totally different. The owner of the company is the person who happens to be holding the share certificate. This means that, provided you do not have the bearer certificates in your possession, you can state that you don't legally own a particular company.

Note the company will still need to pay tax on any profits generated. The only real benefit is in terms of privacy. It would make it more difficult for anyone to argue that you owned a company if bearer shares were used.

Limited Liability Company (LLC)

LLCs are available in a number of jurisdictions, although it has to be said that United States LLCs (in particular the Delaware LLC) are the most popular. The LLC is similar to the UK LLP, although there are some important differences.

Just like an LLP, one of the biggest advantages is pass through taxation. This means that the earnings of the LLC are taxed only once and would be apportioned to the members of the LLC.

Individuals who own an interest in an LLC are known as 'members' as opposed to shareholders.

The LLC structure is known to be very flexible and, in particular, documentary requirements are pretty slack with few requirements to keep minutes or have records of formal resolutions.

It also benefits from limited liability, thus ensuring that your personal assets are kept separate from your business assets.

Unlike an LLP, the minimum number of people needed to form an LLC is one, with a few exceptions. If you did incorporate it with just one member, this would be akin to a one man limited company, albeit with low disclosure and documentary requirements.

If you're a UK resident member of an LLC, you'll be taxed on your share of the profits, although the LLC itself wouldn't be taxed.

Trusts

Trusts were traditionally one of the most popular entities for holding assets. They were particularly useful as they allowed an individual to legally give away assets but still exercise an element of control over them (as a trustee) and in some cases benefit from the assets (as a beneficiary).

In terms of avoiding UK taxes they are much less attractive now than they used to be due to the number of anti-avoidance provisions that operate to negate the tax benefits.

Offshore trusts would usually be used in combination with another entity such as an IBC or a foundation. Typically the trust would be used to hold the shares of an IBC. Alternatively, if a foundation structure was used, the trust could be the beneficiary of the foundation.

Foundations

The use of foundations has gained in popularity over the past few years, given its unique characteristics. The foundation is essentially a cross between a trust and a company because it's a separate legal entity that doesn't have owners.

Foundations are useful because they have a separate legal personality. Therefore when applying for an offshore bank account, it is often necessary to state the beneficial owners. If a foundation is used it is the foundation itself that is the beneficial owner. Foundations are popular primarily for asset protection purposes.

In UK tax terms, they'd be treated in a similar way to a trust.

Protected Cell Companies (PCCs)

Protected cell companies are something of a new development. There are very few jurisdictions that permit them (including Guernsey, Bermuda and Mauritius) and although aimed at big business and the structuring of finance for multinational companies, they could be tailored to a smaller operation if required.

A protected cell company is a company that is split up into different sections. Each section is separate from all the others and rather than simply transferring assets to the company, you transfer assets to the particular cell of the company. Each cell is independent and separate from every other cell.

Therefore, rather than holding assets in separate companies, you could establish one PCC and put different assets in each cell. In terms of any creditors each cell would need to be approached separately and the assets of one cell could not be used to satisfy liabilities of another cell.

They're principally asset protection tools and, given the right circumstances, for example if there is a diverse range of assets involved, they could be useful.

11.10 OVERSEAS TRADING

If you want to do business in another country two of the options you have are:

- Incorporate a new company offshore and use this to carry out the overseas business, or

- Establish a branch of the existing UK company and carry out the trade via the branch.

Note that in physical terms the two would look more or less identical from overseas: there could be overseas premises, staff and equipment.

The main difference would be in the ownership. If the overseas trade was owned by the UK company it would be a branch, if owned by an offshore company it could be a subsidiary.

Deciding whether to use a branch or subsidiary will have significant implications on how the profits from the overseas trade will be taxed.

The main difference between the two is that the profits of a branch will be classed as part of the UK company's taxable profits along with its UK trading profits.

The branch profits will usually be separated from the UK trading income if the branch is actually controlled from overseas, and therefore it could be taxed as income from an overseas 'possession' as opposed to trading income. This difference though is not all that important, and the key point is that the full profits of the overseas branch will be subject to UK corporation tax.

By contrast, if an overseas subsidiary is used, and provided the company is non-UK resident (in other words, the overseas directors exercise control), the profits of the overseas subsidiary should not be subject to UK corporation tax.

As we've seen earlier, the company will be a non-UK resident provided it's not incorporated in the UK, and its central management and control is overseas. In addition, provided the overseas company does not fall within the controlled foreign company provisions (see below) the only time that the UK company will be subject to corporation tax is when the overseas company declares a dividend.

This would therefore give the UK company an element of control over when it incurs a UK tax charge (for example, during an accounting period of otherwise low income).

Another key difference is that if a branch is used and it sustains a loss, this can often be offset against other UK trading profits.

However, if you use an overseas subsidiary and that incurs a loss, the opportunities for it to utilise its loss will be restricted. It could only be used against UK profits where the overseas company is not able to offset the loss against any overseas profits.

An overseas branch could claim tax relief under the capital allowances legislation for assets used in the trade when calculating the taxable profits in the UK company. If you used a subsidiary no capital allowances would be due (unless the overseas country has its own capital allowance rules).

Finally, if you use a subsidiary, this will be classed as another 'associated company' which would reduce the tax bands for calculating the UK company's corporation tax. For example, this could have the effect that the UK company would pay 30% corporation tax on profits exceeding £750,000, as opposed to £1.5 million.

The fact that losses are given more flexible relief in a branch means that, where an overseas operation is expected to incur losses in the first few years of trading, it is often advisable to initially trade overseas using a branch (with full relief for losses in the UK) and then transfer the trade to an overseas subsidiary when it is about to become profitable (to eliminate UK tax on the profits).

11.11 UK CONTROLLED FOREIGN COMPANY (CFC) RULES

I mentioned above that the UK company would not be charged tax on the profits of the overseas non-UK resident subsidiary... provided the UK CFC rules don't apply.

The CFC rules would therefore be of great importance to any company that was looking to establish an overseas subsidiary.

If the CFC rules apply they will ensure that part of the overseas company's profits are taxed in the hands of UK companies who hold an interest in the CFC, provided the percentage of the profits apportioned is at least 25%.

You should note that the UK CFC regime will not apply if you are an individual owning an overseas company.

Before falling within the CFC rules a company would firstly need to meet the definition of a 'controlled foreign company'.

A CFC is defined as:

- A non-UK resident company, and

- A company controlled from the UK, and

- A company subject to overseas tax which is less than 75% of the equivalent UK tax.

Therefore the CFC provisions are going to apply to overseas companies established in low tax countries. What you'd need to do is to calculate the company's profits and find out what the overseas tax charge is.

You'd then calculate the UK tax liability and if the overseas tax paid is less than three-quarters of the UK tax, the overseas company could fall within the CFC provisions.

There are, however, some exemptions available to prevent the CFC rules from applying:

- If the overseas company follows an acceptable distribution policy. This means if the overseas company pays dividends of at least 90% of its profits to the UK company, the profits of the overseas company would not fall within the CFC provisions.

- Low profits. This is a de minimis limit to prevent small companies being brought into charge, so provided taxable profits (excluding gains) are less than £50,000 no tax would arise under the CFC provisions.

- The motive test. Essentially if you can show that a reduction in UK tax was not the main purpose of using the overseas company the CFC provisions will also not apply.

Any UK company that was planning on using an overseas subsidiary would therefore need to be very careful that it didn't fall within the CFC provisions, otherwise it could see the benefits of using an offshore company eliminated.

Chapter 12

Investing in UK Property:
A Case Study

It is useful to consolidate some of the issues covered in previous chapters and consider a typical scenario, where a UK non-resident and non-domiciled individual wishes to purchase a UK property.

Jack is resident and domiciled in Spain. He has relatives in the UK and is interested in purchasing a property here because (a) he wants somewhere to stay when he visits and (b) he has heard that UK property prices are set to rise.

The question is, how from a tax perspective should he structure the purchase?

There are broadly two ways to buy the property:

- By using direct ownership, or
- Using some form of intermediary like a trust or company.

12.1 DIRECT OWNERSHIP

Capital Gains Tax

From a capital gains tax perspective direct ownership is potentially attractive:

- The Principal Private Residence (PPR) relief operates to exempt a gain on the disposal of an individual's main residence. Even if the property is not, on the facts, Jack's main residence, he could certainly submit an election to have it treated as his main residence.

- As he is non-resident, he would not in any case be liable to UK capital gains tax on the disposal of any assets.

Inheritance Tax

The inheritance tax position is, however, not as good. The holding of property in the UK would mean that Jack has a UK estate and, as well as probate being required on his death, the house would be subject to inheritance tax to the extent that the value exceeds the £285,000 nil rate band. As the value of the property is expected to rise rapidly, this could result in a significant tax bill were he to die while still owning the asset. There are, however, a number of methods available to Jack to reduce or eliminate any inheritance tax charge:

Use of multiple ownership

The property could be acquired in multiple ownership. For example, Jack, his wife and children could all own the property jointly.

Provided the individuals have no other UK assets, it is likely that each share will be below the nil rate band.

In order to avoid problems with the 'gift with reservation of benefit' legislation, it is necessary to gift cash to the family members, which they can then use to purchase their shares of the property.

The gift with reservation of benefit (GROB) provisions apply to property in particular, where an interest in a property is given away, yet the person gifting the interest still continues to reside in the property. For inheritance tax purposes, the whole value of the property is still regarded as included in the occupier's estate for inheritance tax purposes.

Gifting of property

Another solution would be to gift cash to a younger member of the family who can then make the acquisition. The gift will be exempt from inheritance tax, provided the person making the gift survives seven years. The above GROB rules would not apply as the gift was a cash gift.

The UK pre-owned assets tax charge should also not be relevant if Jack is non-UK resident.

The property will then belong to the donee (the younger family member) and if the donee were to die, it would be included in his estate for inheritance tax purposes.

Mortgages

The value of an individual's estate is essentially the market value of the assets at the date of death, less any liabilities outstanding at the date of death.

It is therefore possible to effectively reduce any inheritance tax charge to zero, by obtaining a substantial loan against the value of the property. Provided the mortgage reduces the 'net value' of the property to below the nil rate band (currently £285,000) there will be no inheritance tax payable.

The mortgage funds obtained can be invested overseas and any interest return would then be exempt from UK income tax provided the interest income is not remitted to the UK.

12.2   USING A TRUST TO OWN THE PROPERTY

Capital Gains Tax

The Principal Private Residence relief is extended to situations where a beneficiary is entitled to occupy a house under the terms of a trust deed. In these circumstances, the trustees would be able to claim PPR relief when they sell the property.

In the case of a non-UK domiciliary, as the trustees are non-resident they would not, in any case, be liable to UK capital gains tax.

It would only be if the settlor of the trust was also a beneficiary and he acquired a UK domicile that the gains of the trust would be attributed to him under the anti-avoidance provisions.

Inheritance tax

The trust will be subject to special inheritance tax rules. One of the key implications is that it could be subject to an inheritance tax charge every 10 years starting with the date of commencement.

A more serious problem is that HMRC could contend that the non-domiciliary has a 'notional interest in possession' in the property. This is a complex area, however the result of the authorities being successful in this argument would be that the value of the property would be included within the occupier's estate on his death (similar to the effect of the GROB provisions).

One method of avoiding this may be to grant a tenancy at a low or nominal rent, however this is something that would need to be looked at in detail by your professional adviser.

12.3 USING AN OFFSHORE COMPANY

The property could be owned by a non-resident company. In this case the non-domiciliary would own the shares in the company.

As the shares are non-UK property, they would be exempt from inheritance tax. Key risks with this are:

- The company's residence position may be closely scrutinised by the taxman and it may be difficult to show that the central management and control is exercised outside the UK, particularly if all directors are UK resident and the asset of the company is a UK property. If HMRC is able to successfully argue that the company is UK resident, any gain on the disposal of the property would be subject to UK corporation tax and no PPR relief would be available.

- In addition, on a disposal of the shares in the company, no capital gains tax would be payable by Jack provided he remained non-resident. If he was UK resident, he may not be charged to UK CGT provided the proceeds were retained outside the UK, as he's a non-UK domiciliary – again this could be challenged by HMRC by arguing that the central management and control of the company occurred in the UK.

12.4 CONCLUSION

Deciding how a non-domiciliary should own UK property is clearly not a straightforward decision.

Much will depend on the particular circumstances and your personal preferences. For example, you may be more anxious to avoid capital gains tax than inheritance tax.

To a certain extent the simplest route – direct ownership – offers some important tax advantages provided potential inheritance tax can be avoided in some way, for example, by using debt.

Chapter 13

Becoming a Tax Nomad

Just as it is possible to be resident in more than one country, it is also possible to be resident in none. Such individuals are commonly known as 'tax nomads'.

If you become a tax nomad you would still be liable for income tax on any income generated within a particular country, but *capital gains tax* usually depends on the concept of residence.

In order to achieve your objective and pay no capital gains tax, you will need to ensure that you have a thorough understanding of the relevant countries' domestic tax laws, as well as the impact of any double taxation treaties.

The definition of residence varies significantly. Some countries, such as the UK and Ireland, have an objective test, which is determined by the number of days spent within the country.

Other countries, such as France and Germany, have a more subjective test that is based on where an individual's 'centre of economic interest' is located or the place of 'habitual abode'.

Example

Jack spends his time during the tax year 2006/2007 as follows:

- *127 days in Ireland,*
- *84 days a year in the UK,*
- *110 days in the USA,*
- *The remainder of the year on holiday in the Maldives.*

He would not be resident in any of the above countries for tax purposes and this would allow him to avoid a potentially large gain on a disposal of his investment property.

Moving abroad may offer an opportunity to wash out gains in your investment portfolio tax-free, since it may be possible to arrange your move so that for a period you are 'resident nowhere'.

For example, if you move to Spain and leave the UK on 5 April 2007 and travel via France, arriving in Spain on 10 April 2007, any capital gains you realise during the four-day 'tax holiday' between these dates could be free of capital gains tax (unless you resume tax residence in the UK within five years).

Whilst becoming a tax nomad may not be a suitable option long term, it could prove useful for one or two years – it allows you to structure your affairs before taking up residence in a country of your choice.

Chapter 14

Double Tax Treaties

14.1 HOW DOUBLE TAX TREATIES WORK

The rules detailed earlier in this guide explain the concepts of 'residence', 'ordinary residence' and 'domicile' and identify when an individual will be liable to pay UK tax as a result of being resident or ordinarily resident in this country.

But an individual may also be regarded as resident in another country according to its tax laws. This is where double tax treaties come into play.

A double tax treaty is essentially an agreement between two countries that will determine which country has the right to tax you in specified situations. The purpose is to avoid double taxation.

The UK has double tax treaties with a number of countries including popular retirement destinations such as Spain, Portugal, Italy and France.

The majority of the UK's double tax treaties are based on the 'standard' provisions in the model treaty of the OECD (Organisation for Economic Cooperation and Development).

This includes a 'tie-breaker' clause that effectively overrides the two countries' domestic laws and makes the individual resident in one country only. The use of this tie-breaker clause can be extremely beneficial, as we'll see shortly.

14.2 WHAT A TYPICAL DTT LOOKS LIKE

As most of the UK DTTs follow the standard OECD model, I'll explain in the paragraphs that follow what some of the most common OECD double tax treaty provisions are actually trying to achieve.

Some of these are self-explanatory but are worth listing in case you ever want to review a DTT on your own.

Article V – Permanent Establishment

This looks at the definition of a permanent establishment. This is crucial for international traders as this will frequently dictate the extent to which overseas trading activities will be taxable in an overseas jurisdiction. Usually a company trading in the other treaty country would only be taxed on the profits in the 'source' country if they are trading from a permanent establishment located there.

Article VI – Income from Real Property

Typically real property is land and property, so this article would cover the treatment of rental income. As the country where the property is located usually has the initial right to tax, the rental income could easily be taxed in both countries.

Most income tax treaties under Article VI will not avoid this by providing an exemption in one of the countries, so instead you'd usually rely on Article XXIV (elimination of double tax article) to provide a tax credit for the overseas tax suffered (see below).

Article XI – Interest

This looks at the position where interest is paid by a resident of one country to a resident of another. The treaty between the two countries would usually look to reduce any withholding taxes (for example, in the case of the UK it would identify if the UK 20% withholding tax would be reduced).

Article XIII – Capital Gains

This is the one that is of most importance for property investors looking to emigrate and sell up. It covers capital gains from the disposal of assets and seeks to reduce the tax dependent on the specific treaty country. In many cases there is a standard provision that capital gains remain taxable only in the owner's country of residence, except for land and property which can also usually be taxed in the country where the property is located. So whilst most expats could be exempt from UK taxes, they could find themselves liable to capital gains tax overseas.

Article XIV – Independent Personal Services

This looks at the taxation of income from self-employed people and again will generally look to whether the individual has a 'fixed base' overseas. If they do, then it's often only the profits generated by this fixed base that can be taxed overseas.

Article XV – Dependent Personal Services

This looks at the taxation of employment income. In many treaties if the income is paid and borne by a foreign employer and the employee is not physically present in the UK for more than 183 days, the income will only be taxable in the employee's country of residence.

Article XXII – Other Income

This looks at the taxation of all other income not addressed elsewhere and usually gives sole taxing rights to the country of residence.

Article XXIV – Elimination of Double Taxation

This provides for double tax relief, so that even if income is taxed twice you'll be able to deduct overseas tax that you've suffered from any UK liability. Although useful, the UK would usually provide for double tax relief anyway, even if there was no treaty in place (under what is known as 'unilateral relief').

Exceptionally, some treaties may also grant an exemption rather than the credit method above (for example, the current UK-France treaty has an exemption provision for certain purposes, but the new treaty will change to a credit method).

Article XXVII – Exchange of Information

This is an agreement between the two tax authorities to allow them to share information, mainly to avoid tax evasion. This is the other side to double tax treaties – as well as looking to reduce tax, they are also effectively information exchange agreements.

The terms of double tax treaties can therefore be immensely complex, although on a simple level they can provide for one country to have primary taxing rights over certain sources of income and gains.

The tie-breaker clause that I mentioned earlier is the way that the tax treaty will determine in which of the two countries an individual is resident for treaty purposes.

A typical treaty would provide that:

- If you have a permanent home in one state, you are resident in that state.

- If you have a permanent home in both states, you are resident in the state that is your 'centre of vital interests' – the country in which you have close personal and financial ties.

- If you do not have a permanent home in either state and it is not possible to determine your centre of vital interests, you are resident in the country where you have an 'habitual abode'.

One important point to note is that there are very few low-tax countries that have double tax treaties with the UK. The UK has, however, concluded double tax treaties with the Channel Islands and the Isle of Man, which are low-tax jurisdictions. The UK-Isle of Man double tax treaty is looked at in more detail below.

It is also crucial to note that for the tie-breaker clause to apply, you must be resident in two countries under the terms of each country's domestic laws. The treaty cannot make you resident in a country if you are not already resident under the domestic law of that country.

There is also a tie breaker clause for companies, which usually looks at the country where the 'effective management is carried out'. Before this could apply a company would need to be resident in both treaty countries. For example, in the *Wood v Holden* case mentioned previously, HMRC argued that the Dutch company was UK resident given its central management and control was in the UK.

HMRC also said that under the UK-Netherlands tax treaty the company was UK resident as the effective place of management was not in the Netherlands. However, as the High Court judge ruled that the company was Dutch resident, the treaty provision was not relevant in deciding the company's residence.

Note that I'm not saying that you need to be resident in both treaty countries to obtain the benefits under the treaty, just that the residence tie-breaker rules won't apply unless you are dual resident.

The other provisions relating to income and gains will usually apply where you have a potential tax charge in both states. Therefore you could be UK resident but if you invest in German property you'll be subject to both countries' capital gains tax regime and will look to the treaty to identify how this deals with the double taxation.

14.3   THE UK-ISLE OF MAN DOUBLE TAX TREATY

The Isle of Man (IOM) has only one Double Taxation Agreement which was entered into with the United Kingdom in 1955 and is very similar to agreements drawn up between the UK and Jersey and Guernsey.

The treaty does not conform to the OECD standard model treaty and is of limited scope. The main features that may be of interest are the following:

- The agreement applies only for income tax purposes (in both the IOM and the UK).

- An individual resident in only one of the two countries is exempt from tax in the other country on personal, including professional, services performed in the other country on behalf of a resident of his own country (but they must be taxed in his own country). In other words, if you are a resident of the IOM and perform services in the UK for a UK resident individual, then provided the income was taxed in the IOM, there would be no UK tax liability.

If these criteria are not met then tax would be payable in both countries, although the tax paid in one country is allowed as a credit against tax due in the other. If you did incur UK tax whilst being an IOM resident, the UK tax paid would be offset against any IOM tax.

Given that UK income tax rates are generally significantly higher then IOM rates, this would extinguish any IOM income tax liability.

It is important to note that capital gains tax is not subject to the double tax treaty.

Why the Isle of Man is So Attractive

Tax rates are much lower in the Isle of Man than in the UK.

Income tax is levied at a rate of only 10% on the first £10,500 of taxable income and 18% on the rest. Individuals receive an £8,670 personal allowance. Married couples are taxed jointly and receive a personal allowance of £17,340, pay 10% on the first £21,000 of taxable income and 18% on the rest. The Isle of Man has also recently introduced an income tax liability cap of £100,000. This means that if you're a very wealthy person, your maximum income tax charge is restricted to £100,000.

National Insurance is a form of social security taxation. It is levied on employment income at an identical rate to the UK. For employees the rate is 11% on income between £97 and £645 per week.

Rates are a form of property tax and are based on a notional house value multiplied by a formula set by the local authority.

VAT is charged at 17.5% on the value of an item. There are some variations, but generally the tax is applied in a similar manner to the UK.

There is no capital gains tax in the Isle of Man.

How to Become Resident in the Isle of Man

There is no general definition of 'residence' or 'ordinary residence' in Manx tax law – these terms are often interpreted in the same way as in English law.

A person will qualify as a resident if he spends a total of six months on the island in any income tax year (April 6th to April 5th). An individual who visits for more than an average of three months each year for four or more consecutive years will also be deemed resident. There is an important short-term residence concession which allows a person who owns a property on the island to spend not more than four months in any two consecutive years in the island and not be liable to Manx income tax.

A new resident is taxed from the date of arrival, while a person who leaves is non-resident from the date of departure. Resident individuals are liable to tax on their worldwide income, non-residents only on income arising on the island.

14.4   USING DOUBLE TAX TREATIES TO SAVE TAX

Before the 2005 Budget it was possible to use certain favourable double tax treaties with countries like Belgium, Portugal and New Zealand to avoid having to leave the UK for five years to avoid capital gains tax.

These treaties superseded the UK domestic tax legislation and allowed only the overseas country to tax gains of residents, thus preventing a UK tax charge, even if the person became UK resident within five years.

However, this is no longer possible due to the new anti-avoidance rules. The fact that a double tax treaty exists does not prevent UK Revenue and Customs taxing any gain arising in the tax year of your return.

You would therefore need to actually remain resident overseas for a five-year period for the gain to be exempt from UK capital gains tax.

If this is an option (for example, if the amount of any gain is significant) you could choose a CGT-free destination such as the Isle of Man or the Channel Islands, a complete tax haven such as Monaco, or a country that has specific provisions to exempt gains on overseas property (for example, Cyprus).

After the tax year of disposal, you could then cease to be a resident of this country and travel or establish residence in another country of your choice (for example, Spain). Provided you do not become a UK resident for five complete tax years, you will be exempt from UK CGT. You could return to the UK for visits of up to 90 days per tax year, although you should keep these to a minimum, particularly if you have UK family or property.

Although the use of double tax treaties to avoid UK capital gains tax has decreased, the use of treaties for individuals and companies to avoid income tax or corporation tax is still significant. For example, the permanent establishment provisions of a relevant double tax treaty are very important for international traders as they can actively limit liability to UK taxes for UK resident traders.

14.5   TREATY RELIEF

Remember that double tax treaties override domestic tax legislation. In the standard OECD model tax treaty, dividends are taxed in the country of residence, as opposed to the country where the company is resident.

Example

Peter is a resident of South Africa. He holds shares in a UK resident company and receives dividends twice yearly (interim and final dividends). Under the UK-South Africa double tax treaty, the dividends will be taxed solely in South Africa.

Similarly, interest is also taxed in the country where the individual is resident. If in the above example Peter received interest from a

UK bank, as a South African resident the treaty now exempts the UK source interest from UK tax.

However, interest is automatically paid net, as income tax of 20% is withheld by the bank. In this case, you would need to contact Revenue and Customs and apply for treaty relief in order that the exemption from UK tax can apply. This would then allow a repayment of any tax withheld, and would ensure that no income tax is deducted on future payments.

Claiming treaty relief can be a long process. The form, which can be obtained from Revenue and Customs (www.hmrc.gov.uk/cnr/), must be completed and passed to the overseas revenue service. It will then review the information and pass this back to the UK HMRC where the Centre for Non Residents will issue a certificate granting relief.

14.6   CONSIDERING A MOVE TO SPAIN

Let's have a look at Spain, a popular destination for potential expats. Whilst Spain does not offer low tax rates, it still remains a popular choice for UK emigrants due to its proximity to the UK, fantastic climate and political stability.

Those who either purchase Spanish assets or acquire Spanish residence will be affected by the local tax regime so it's worth examining in greater detail.

We shall give a brief overview of the Spanish tax regime below. This will highlight the similarities and differences between the two countries, before looking at how the UK-Spain double tax treaty affects matters.

Residence

The extent that you are liable to these taxes will depend on your residence position. You will either be UK resident or Spanish resident (assuming you live and split your time between the UK and Spain).

Residence is important because UK and Spanish residents are taxed on their *worldwide* income and gains, whereas non-residents are only liable to tax on the income arising within that particular country. For example, non-UK residents are only liable to UK income tax on their UK income.

Spanish Residence

The first point to note is that the Spanish tax year is based on calendar years, unlike our tax year which runs from 6th April to 5th April. There are numerous rules regarding different levels of status in Spain:

- Individuals who spend more than 183 days in Spain during one calendar year must apply for a Spanish resident card, and be classed as permanent residents. These days do not have to be consecutive. You do not become a resident for tax purposes until the morning of the 184th day.

- Temporary absences from Spain are ignored for the purpose of this rule unless it can be proved that the individual is habitually resident in another country for more than 183 days in a calendar year.

- If you arrive in Spain with the intention of living there indefinitely, the Spanish tax authorities (known as the 'Hacienda') will treat you as Spanish resident from the day after your arrival.

- If your spouse lives in Spain, you will be presumed to be a resident of Spain, provided you are not separated/divorced even though you may actually spend fewer than 183 days per year in Spain.

If you live on a boat within 12 nautical miles of Spanish land, you are classed as a Spanish tax resident. A day within 12 nautical miles is a day spent in Spain for tax purposes.

It is clear that following the UK and Spanish domestic residence rules (above) an individual can be resident in both the UK and Spain. This is where it is important to identify how the double taxation agreement regulates matters.

How Does the UK/Spain Treaty Affect Matters?

The UK/Spain Double Tax Treaty has a 'tie-breaker' clause that comes into effect if an individual is classed as resident in the UK and Spain (under the domestic rules outlined above). This clause determines which country is to be given sole taxing rights, and prevents an individual being subject to UK and Spanish taxes on the same income. The double tax agreement states that:

- If an individual is resident in both Spain and the UK, according to the domestic tax rules, he is to be deemed resident in the country in which he has a permanent home.

- If he has permanent homes in both Spain and the UK, he is deemed to be resident in the country that is classed as his centre of vital interests. This is a vague term, although it is generally regarded as the country with which an individual has the strongest ties and will therefore include both personal and financial connections.

- If it is still not possible to determine which country has the taxing rights, it is necessary to look at the individual's habitual abode – the country in which he has his habitual abode (which is similar to the concept of main residence) will be his country of residence.

- If he has an habitual abode in the UK and Spain, he will be resident in the country in which he is a national.

Example

Bob, a UK resident, owns a villa in Spain. If he occupies the villa for three months he will be a UK (not Spanish) resident, liable to UK income tax. If Bob rents out the villa, both the UK and Spanish tax authorities are likely to want a piece of the action. Although non-resident in Spain, Bob's rental income will have a Spanish source and so Spanish tax will be payable. The UK tax authorities will be interested because Bob is UK resident, therefore subject to UK income tax on his worldwide income. In this case, the UK-Spain double tax treaty gives both countries the right to tax the income, so Bob will pay UK income tax and Spanish income tax (at the non-resident rate of 25% on the gross income, with no deductions for expenses or interest costs). Bob needs to keep copies of his Spanish tax returns so he can offset the Spanish tax against any UK liability.

Assuming that Bob is a UK higher-rate taxpayer, and receives rental income of £10,000 and incurs costs of £2,000. The Spanish income tax liability would be £2,500 (£10,000 x 25%). UK tax would be £10,000 - £2,000 x 40% = £3,200.

Bob would then be entitled to deduct the Spanish income tax paid from the UK income tax. The net effect of this is that Bob would actually pay £3,200 in income tax on the villa (£2,500 in Spain and £700 in the UK).

What Else Does the Double Tax Treaty Say?

The treaty has specific rules that will apply to certain types of income, irrespective of the domestic tax laws of the UK or Spain.

Under the domestic tax legislation of the UK and Spain it is easily possible for income to fall within the UK and Spanish tax systems. This is clearly unfair, and both the UK and Spain provide for a system of double tax relief where there is an element of double taxation.

However, in order to minimise this double tax the treaty has specifically stated in which country certain types of income will be taxed, when both countries may have a claim on the same income. The summarised rules are as follows:

Rental Income

The general rule is that this is taxed in the country where you are resident. Therefore once you become a resident in Spain, you will have to pay income tax on the rental income to the Spanish revenue authorities. However, the treaty also states that "income from immovable property... may be taxed in the Contracting State in which such property is situated".

In the case of a Spanish resident owning UK property, you would therefore still have to pay income tax on the rental income you derive from your UK property to UK Revenue and Customs. The non-resident landlord scheme, which forces tenants and letting agents to pay over tax on behalf of overseas property owners, would then apply to collect UK tax. This means that you would pay tax in the UK as well as Spain, but would look to double tax relief to claim a deduction for the UK tax suffered. This would then prevent the rental income being taxed twice.

Dividends, Interest and Pension Income

The dividend and interest provisions give the primary right to tax dividends and interest to the country where the recipient is resident. Therefore a Spanish resident individual receiving dividend income or interest from a UK resident company or bank would pay income tax in Spain under the terms of the double taxation agreement.

The treaty would also allow the UK to tax the income if it wished (subject to some limitations). However, as we've seen under the UK tax rules, there would usually be no UK tax liability on UK-sourced dividends or bank interest for a non-UK resident.

Pensions, apart from Government Service Pensions, are specifically stated to be only taxable in the country of residence. This is provided by Article 18 of the UK-Spain double tax treaty which states:

"(1) Subject to the provisions of Article 19 pensions and other similar remuneration paid in consideration of past employment to a resident of a Contracting State and any annuity paid to such a resident shall be taxable only in that State."

Therefore a non-governmental pension paid from the UK to a Spanish resident would not be subject to UK income tax. If the pension was from the UK Government (for example, if you worked as a civil servant or a police officer etc) it would then, however, be taxed only in the UK (unless you were both a Spanish resident and a Spanish national, in which case it would again be taxable only in Spain).

Property Capital Gains

These are taxed in the country where the property is situated, as well as the country of residence. However most expats disposing of a UK property would be exempt from UK capital gains tax provided they satisfied the UK rules (for example, non-resident and not ordinarily resident for five complete tax years). In this case the tax liability would therefore primarily be a Spanish liability and this would usually be at a rate of 15%.

You will see that whilst the domestic concepts of residence for UK and Spain are important, the double tax treaty certainly simplifies matters, as it basically tells us which country's rules to use. When considering a move to any country you should consider whether a double tax treaty exists and how this will impact on the tax treatment of income and gains.

Other Countries' Treatment of Capital Gains

Most countries adopt similar provisions to those above, with the result that both the UK and the overseas country would have taxing rights over capital gains.

One of the few treaties that doesn't apply this rule is the one between the UK and Greece. This states:

"A resident of one of the territories who does not carry on a trade or business in the other territory through a permanent establishment situated therein shall be exempt in that other territory from any tax on gains from the sale, transfer or exchange of capital assets."

Therefore the effect of this would be that if you are a resident of Greece and own UK property you would not be subject to UK CGT when you sell the property. Of course, in most cases this will not be important because if you are a resident of Greece you'd be non-UK resident and possibly exempt from UK capital gains tax.

The main use of the Greece treaty used to be to avoid the five-year absence rule for UK capital gains. However, as we've seen, this rule has now been amended so that it cannot be circumvented by using a double tax treaty.

If you are serious about avoiding both UK and overseas tax on the disposal of UK properties you need to satisfy the five-year requirement to gain a UK capital gains tax exemption. You also have to ensure that you are a resident of an overseas country that itself would not tax the gain.

There are different ways that you can avoid paying taxes overseas. The overseas country may simply levy no taxes at all, or it may levy income tax but not capital gains tax, or it may apply a territorial basis and just tax local income and gains. There are lots of countries that could be used to avoid tax on any UK property investment gains including the Caribbean tax havens, Cyprus, the Isle of Man, Malta, and Monaco. We've covered these in more detail in our overseas tax guide, *The World's Best Tax Havens*.

If you weren't disposing of land or property, but were looking at a disposal of shares, the treatment in the double tax treaty would vary a lot more.

The UK-France treaty, for instance, states:

"...Gains from the alienation of any property other than that referred to in paragraphs (1) and (2) (paragraphs 1 and 2 relate to land and property) *shall be taxable only in the Contracting State in which the alienator is resident.*

(4) Notwithstanding the provisions of paragraph (3), gains derived by an individual who is a resident of a Contracting State from the alienation of more than 25% of the shares held, alone or together with related persons, directly or indirectly, in a company which is a resident of the other Contracting State may be taxed in that other State. The provisions of this paragraph shall only apply if:

(a) the individual is a national of the other Contracting State without also being a national of the first-mentioned Contracting State; and

(b) the individual has been a resident of the other Contracting State at any time in a five year period immediately preceding the alienation of the shares..."

Therefore, if you're a French resident but are a UK national and have been a UK resident at any time in the previous five years and you sell more than 25% of the shares held in a UK company, you could be taxed in the UK. As stated previously, the five-year residence exemption would apply anyway. You'd be subject to French taxes, though, on the basis you were a French resident.

By contrast, the UK-Denmark treaty doesn't expressly cover the position of a disposal of shares and states:

"...Gains from the alienation of any property other than that referred to in paragraphs (1), (2), (3) and (4) of this Article, shall be taxable only in the Contracting State of which the alienator is a resident..."

Therefore this would allocate sole taxing rights over the shares disposal to Denmark. In both cases the overseas country of residence would obtain a right to tax the gain, the difference is that in the latter the treaty would only allow Denmark to tax the gain unless you went back to the UK without satisfying the five-year absence rule.

The interpretation of double tax treaties is a complex area, and you should always take advice from an international tax specialist.

Chapter 15

Buying Property Abroad

15.1 INTRODUCTION

A lot of UK property investors are thinking about buying property abroad. Many are interested in the emerging markets of Eastern Europe (Latvia, Poland, Bulgaria and the like). Others stick to traditional favourites such as France, Italy and Spain.

There is a tendency amongst investors to get caught up in the excitement of owning an overseas property and neglect certain important financial issues, such as how any income and capital gains will be taxed.

The UK tax treatment will depend primarily on the tax status of the purchaser. Let's have a look at the UK tax implications for different types of purchaser, pooling together what we've learned in previous chapters.

15.2 UK RESIDENT/ORDINARILY RESIDENT AND DOMICILED

Any income and gains arising from the property will in the first instance be liable to UK taxes in full. The property will also be included within your estate for inheritance tax purposes.

Example

Jake is resident and domiciled in the UK. He decides to purchase a property in Latvia for letting during the summer months and for his own occupation during the winter. The rental income will be subject to UK income tax. Any gain/profit on a subsequent disposal will be liable to UK capital gains tax (less various reliefs). If he were to die whilst still owning the Latvian property, this would be taken into account when assessing the amount of inheritance tax he would pay.

15.3 NON-RESIDENT/ORDINARILY RESIDENT AND NON-UK DOMICILED

As you would expect, as a non-resident, any income and gains from the overseas property will not be liable to UK taxes. Similarly, the property would not be included within the individual's estate for inheritance tax purposes.

Example

Jacob, originally born in Portugal, has lived in Spain for 15 years and is regarded as non-UK resident and non-UK domiciled. His Spanish property would not be subject to UK taxes.

Note that for capital gains tax purposes, an individual must be non-resident for five complete tax years before being exempted from UK capital gains tax on assets held at the date of their emigration.

This provision was enacted in 1998 to prevent people with large potential gains in assets, becoming non-resident for a tax year, disposing of the asset and avoiding UK capital gains tax.

15.4 UK RESIDENT/ORDINARILY RESIDENT AND NON-UK DOMICILED

Individuals who are UK resident but non-UK domiciled have a number of advantages when it comes to UK taxes. Such individuals are typically foreign nationals (usually born overseas) who have come to live in the UK for a number of years.

The key aspect will be that for income tax and capital gains tax the remittance basis applies. This means that any rental income from overseas property would be exempt from UK taxes provided the income is not remitted to the UK. In addition, on a future disposal no UK capital gains tax would be payable provided the sale proceeds are retained overseas.

Again, from a UK tax perspective, there would be no UK inheritance tax impact. As a non-UK domiciliary, your estate would include only UK assets.

Example

Petra has lived in the UK for 10 years but has retained her overseas domicile. Petra has purchased a property in Monaco. She plans to rent this out for two years and then dispose of it for a (hopefully!) significant profit.

Provided Petra retains the income overseas (for example, in an offshore bank account) and doesn't bring it into the UK, there will be no UK income tax charge. The same principle will apply to the sale proceeds. This will allow Petra to build up a tax-free amount that she could use to purchase further offshore properties.

Similarly, the property would not be classed as part of Petra's estate for inheritance tax purposes (being non-UK property of a non-UK domiciliary).

One point to watch out for are the 'deemed domicile' rules. These apply for inheritance tax purposes only and state that individuals are deemed to have a UK domicile:

- If they have been UK resident for 17 out of the last 20 years, or
- They have lost their UK domicile in the last three years.

Example

In the above example, assume Petra has been living in the UK since 1970. For income tax purposes and capital gains tax purposes, Petra is of non-UK domicile. However, for inheritance tax purposes, she is deemed UK domicile as she has lived in the UK since 1970 and would therefore have been resident for more than 17 years.

Therefore for inheritance tax purposes, Petra would be subject to UK inheritance tax on her worldwide estate. This would mean that the property in Monaco could potentially be subject to UK inheritance tax.

Non-UK domiciliaries have a useful tax advantage when considering investing in overseas property. Provided they reinvest income and proceeds offshore, they can avoid UK taxes. This could result in a significant increase in the size and value of their investment portfolios as it enables them to reinvest in more overseas properties. This can give a useful boost to an offshore property portfolio.

15.5   USE OF AN OFFSHORE COMPANY/TRUST

A common misconception is that an offshore company or trust can be used in virtually all situations to avoid UK taxes. Unfortunately this is not true. For UK resident and domiciled individuals the UK tax authorities have a number of powerful anti-avoidance measures at their disposal.

This essentially allows the taxman to deem income to be subject to UK tax in a number of situations. It is therefore only in a number of limited situations that UK residents and domiciliaries can use offshore companies/trusts to avoid UK taxes.

Non-UK domiciliaries can, however, make good use of offshore trusts to purchase overseas property. The trust would not be subject to UK inheritance tax as the assets of the trust would be overseas assets.

From a capital gains tax perspective, the trustees would not be liable to UK capital gains tax, as the trust would be non-resident. Provided the creator of the trust retains his non-UK domicile status, the UK anti-avoidance provisions attributing/deeming gains would not apply.

Provided the overseas jurisdiction does not levy capital gains tax, there would also be no overseas tax charge (for example in the Isle of Man).

Another useful opportunity for the non-UK domiciliary is to ensure that UK assets are owned by a non-resident company, of which the non-domiciliary is a 100% shareholder.

This would then ensure that the individual owns offshore assets (exempt from inheritance tax for non-UK domiciliaries) as opposed to UK assets (charged to UK inheritance tax).

15.6   USING MIXED RESIDENCE PARTNERSHIPS TO AVOID CGT

Another option that could be considered is using a partnership.

There are occasions where a UK resident (individual A) is looking to invest in overseas property but may also have a *non-resident* friend, relative or business partner (individual B) who will be undertaking the investment with them. The question is how should they structure the property purchases?

They could keep the purchases in the name of the non-resident. As a non-resident and not ordinarily resident individual, B would be outside the scope of UK capital gains tax. A, as a UK resident individual, would be subject to CGT on any gains arising. The problem with this arrangement is that it is unlikely to be commercially acceptable to A, who would want to have some entitlement to the assets.

A further problem is that, for tax purposes, HMRC would look to the *beneficial* ownership of the property as opposed to the strict legal ownership. Therefore even if title was solely in B's name, if A would be entitled to a share of any rental income and proceeds of disposal there is a risk that HMRC could assess a share of the gain on A in any case, and therefore UK capital gains tax would be charged.

This is where a partnership may be beneficial. If they were to use a partnership structure the general rule is that each partner would be assessed on their share of the partnership's profits and gains. In this case, however, the partnership would be a mixed residence partnership (as B would be non-resident, and A would be UK resident). This complicates matters and special rules relating to mixed residence partnerships would need to be considered.

In this case it would be necessary to look at the control and management of the partnership (in a similar way that HMRC would look to see if an offshore company was controlled from the UK). If the control and management of a partnership carrying on a trade or business is situated outside the UK the business is deemed to be carried on by individuals not resident in the UK. For CGT purposes, a partner in such a partnership is treated as if he were not resident in the UK (but only in relation to disposals of that partnership's assets).

Therefore, provided they could show the management and control of the partnership was overseas, and that the partnership was engaged in a business, for capital

gains tax purposes, both A and B should be exempt from UK capital gains tax. Note that in terms of any rental profit, A would still be within the scope of UK income tax.

Establishing an overseas residence for the partnership would be a complex area. However, as when looking at the residence of an overseas company, HMRC would tend to look at the place of the highest level of management rather than day-to-day management.

They would usually look at factors such as the location of partners' meetings, the seniority of the partners in age and experience and where major transactions were undertaken.

A and B could also consider having equal capital sharing ratios (to split capital equally) but giving the non-resident partner a higher profit sharing ratio to increase his interest in the partnership and possibly increase the likelihood of establishing the partnership offshore.

Any planning involving using an offshore partnership would need to be carefully considered with your professional adviser.

15.7   WHAT ABOUT OVERSEAS TAX IMPLICATIONS?

Of course the downside to all of the above is that we have only looked at the UK tax implications. Many countries retain the right to tax:

- Residents, and
- Assets of non-residents located within their jurisdiction.

Therefore, anyone considering purchasing a property overseas should take advice from a relevant tax professional as to how any income or gain will be taxed locally.

In the case of Spain, for example, UK resident individuals are taxed at a standard 35% on any gains arising on a disposal and 25% on the gross rental income.

In addition, the 'standard' double tax treaty that most countries choose to adopt would treat the income/gain as being sourced from the country in which the property is located and therefore subject to the overseas tax regime. It would therefore only be if a property was purchased in a 'tax haven' that liability could be avoided. Such tax havens include Andorra, Monaco, and the Cayman Islands.

15.8   DOUBLE TAX RELIEF (DTR)

If you are subject to tax both in the UK and overseas, there are provisions designed to ensure that you don't pay tax twice. As mentioned earlier this is known as double tax relief (DTR) and you can claim DTR against your UK tax charge.

DTR is given as the lower of:

- The UK tax on the overseas income
- The overseas tax

Therefore, if the overseas tax was charged at 50%, with UK tax being 40%, you would obtain DTR at 40%. Similarly, if the overseas tax was charged at 20% and UK tax 40%, you would only obtain DTR at 20%. The net effect of this is that you will be left paying the highest tax charge.

Example

Richard, a UK resident individual has the following income in the 2006/2007 tax year:

UK salary	*£40,000*
UK dividends (gross)	*£2,000*
Overseas rental income	*£3,000*
(50% overseas tax paid)	

His tax calculation would be:	
Salary from UK employment	*£40,000*
Overseas income	*£3,000*
UK dividends	*£2,000*
Less personal allowance	*(£5,035)*
Taxable income	*£39,965*

The income tax levied on this taxable income would be reduced by double tax relief.

As the overseas income will be subject to tax at the higher rate (as the taxable income exceeds the UK higher rate tax band), we can calculate that the double tax relief will be the lower of

- *The UK tax on overseas income (40% x £3,000) = £1,200*
- *The overseas tax (50% x £3,000) = £1,500*

Therefore total double tax relief in this case would be £1,200 (lowest of the two figures) and this would be given as a credit against Richard's tax liability.

15.9   SUMMARY

The tax implications of purchasing a property overseas are certainly not straightforward and you should always consider carefully the UK and (just as importantly) the overseas tax implications.

By way of a summary, I would suggest that the following points be borne in mind when purchasing a property overseas:

- Assess your residence/domicile position to ascertain your liability to UK taxes.

- Obtain overseas tax advice to determine what rate of taxes (if any) exist overseas.

- Retain all receipts (for example, conveyancing fees, valuations, agency fees) – these can be offset when calculating any gain charged to UK capital gains tax.

- Keep full information/documentation of any tax suffered on overseas income/gains – this will be required to substantiate a DTR claim, should HMRC ask questions after you submit your tax return.

- Think about the most effective structure for the purchase, whether this be by you individually or via a company or trust.

- If you are a non-UK domiciliary, watch out for the deemed domicile rules and consider getting advice from a professional about establishing an offshore trust. It's best to do this sooner rather than later. It is the status of the trust creator at the date the trust is established that is crucial for inheritance tax purposes (and will be for capital gains tax and income tax purposes after 6 April 2007). If you later became a UK domiciliary, the trust assets would still be exempt from UK inheritance tax.

Appendix: UK-Spain Double Tax Treaty

ARTICLE 13 UK SPAIN DOUBLE TAX TREATY

(1) Capital gains from the alienation of immovable property, as defined in paragraph (2) of Article 6, may be taxed in the Contracting State in which such property is situated.

(2) Capital gains from the alienation of movable property forming part of the business property of a permanent establishment which an enterprise of a Contracting State has in the other Contracting State or of movable property pertaining to a fixed base available to a resident of a Contracting State in the other Contracting State for the purpose of performing professional services, including such gains from the alienation of such a permanent establishment (alone or together with the whole enterprise) or of such a fixed base, may be taxed in the other State.

(3) Notwithstanding the provisions of paragraph (2) of this Article, capital gains derived by a resident of a Contracting State from the alienation of ships and aircraft operated in international traffic and movable property pertaining to the operation of such ships and aircraft shall be taxable only in that Contracting State.

(4) Capital gains from the alienation of any property other than those mentioned in paragraphs (1), (2) and (3) of this Article shall be taxable only in the Contracting State of which the alienator is a resident.

ARTICLE 24(4)

Income and capital gains owned by a resident of a Contracting State which may be taxed in the other Contracting State in accordance with this Convention shall be deemed to arise from sources in that other Contracting State.

Need Affordable Tax Planning Guidance?

Try Our Unique Question & Answer Service

The purpose of this guide is to provide you with detailed guidance on how to pay less UK tax if you become non-resident or use offshore tax planning techniques.

Ultimately you may want to take further action or obtain guidance personal to your circumstances.

Taxcafe.co.uk has a unique online tax service that provides access to highly qualified tax professionals at an affordable rate.

No matter how complex your question, we will provide you with detailed tax planning guidance through this service. The cost is just £69.95.

To find out more go to **www.taxcafe.co.uk** and click the Tax Questions button.

TAX Cafe™

Pay Less Tax!

... with help from Taxcafe's unique tax guides and software

All products available online at www.taxcafe.co.uk

- ➤ **How to Avoid Property Tax** - Essential reading for property investors who want to know all the tips and tricks to follow to pay less tax on their property profits.

- ➤ **Using a Property Company to Save Tax** - How to massively increase your profits by using a property company... plus all the traps to avoid.

- ➤ **How to Avoid Inheritance Tax** - A-Z of inheritance tax planning, with clear explanations and numerous examples. Covers simple and sophisticated tax planning.

- ➤ **Tax Planning for Couples** - How married and unmarried couples can save thousands in income tax, capital gains tax, inheritance tax and national insurance using a variety of powerful tax planning techniques.

- ➤ **Non Resident & Offshore Tax Planning** - How to exploit non-resident tax status to reduce your tax bill, plus advice on using offshore trusts and companies.

- ➤ **The World's Best Tax Havens** – How to cut your taxes to zero and safeguard your financial freedom.

- ➤ **How to Avoid Stamp Duty** - Little known but perfectly legal trade secrets to reduce your stamp duty bill when buying or selling property.

- ➤ **Grow Rich with a Property ISA** - Find out how to invest in property tax free with an ISA.

- ➢ **Using a Company to Save Tax** - Everything you need to know about the tax benefits of using a company to run your business.

- ➢ **Bonus vs Dividend** - Shows how shareholder/directors of companies can save thousands in tax by choosing the optimal mix of bonus and dividend.

- ➢ **How to Avoid Tax on Your Stock Market Profits** - How to pay less capital gains tax, income tax and inheritance tax on your stock market investments and dealings.

- ➢ **Selling a Sole Trader Business** - A potential minefield with numerous traps to avoid but significant tax-saving opportunities.

- ➢ **How to Claim Tax Credits** - Even families with higher incomes can make successful tax credit claims. This guide shows how much you can claim and how to go about it.

- ➢ **Property Capital Gains Tax Calculator** - Unique software that performs complex capital gains tax calculations in seconds.

Printed in the United Kingdom
by Lightning Source UK Ltd.
128571UK00001B/295/A